The Art of Songwriting

TITLES IN THIS SERIES INCLUDE:

The History of Alternative Rock

The History of American Pop

The History of the Blues

The History of Classical Music

The History of Country Music

The History of Gospel Music

The History of Jazz

The History of Latin Music

The History of Music Videos

The History of R&B and Soul

The History of Rap and Hip-Hop

The History of Rock and Roll

The Instruments of Music

The Art of Songwriting

JENNY MACKAY

LUCENT BOOKS
A part of Gale, Cengage Learning

GALE
CENGAGE Learning™

Detroit • New York • San Francisco • New Haven, Conn • Waterville, Maine • London

LIBRARY OF CONGRESS CATALOGING-IN-PUBLICATION DATA

MacKay, Jenny, 1978-
    The art of songwriting / by Jenny MacKay.
        pages cm. -- (The music library)
    Includes bibliographical references and index.
    ISBN 978-1-4205-0943-4 (hardcover)
    1. Popular music--Writing and publishing--Juvenile literature. I. Title.
    MT67.M15 2014
    782.42'13--dc23
                                    2013022287

Lucent Books
27500 Drake Rd
Farmington Hills MI 48331

ISBN-13: 978-1-4205-0943-4
ISBN-10: 1-4205-0943-8

Printed in the United States of America
1 2 3 4 5 6 7 17 16 15 14 13

CONTENTS

Foreword   6

Introduction
The Culture of Writing in Song   8

Chapter 1
The History of American Pop Music   12

Chapter 2
Melody, Harmony, and Rhythm   31

Chapter 3
All in the Words   48

Chapter 4
Putting the Pieces of a Song Together   63

Chapter 5
The Business of Songwriting   80

Notes   96
Recommended Listening   100
Glossary   104
For More Information   105
Index   107
Picture Credits   111
About the Author   112

In the nineteenth century, English novelist Charles Kingsley wrote, "Music speaks straight to our hearts and spirits, to the very core and root of our souls. . . . Music soothes us, stirs us up . . . melts us to tears." As Kingsley stated, music is much more than just a pleasant arrangement of sounds. It is the resonance of emotion, a joyful noise, a human endeavor that can soothe the spirit or excite the soul. Musicians can also imitate the expressive palette of the earth, from the violent fury of a hurricane to the gentle flow of a babbling brook.

The word *music* is derived from the fabled Greek muses, the children of Apollo who ruled the realms of inspiration and imagination. Composers have long called upon the muses for help and insight. Music is not merely the result of emotions and pleasurable sensations, however.

Music is a discipline subject to formal study and analysis. It involves the juxtaposition of creative elements such as rhythm, melody, and harmony with intellectual aspects of composition, theory, and instrumentation. Like painters mixing red, blue, and yellow into thousands of colors, musicians blend these various elements to create classical symphonies, jazz improvisations, country ballads, and rock-and-roll tunes.

Throughout centuries of musical history, individual musical elements have been blended and modified in infinite ways. The resulting sounds may convey a whole range of moods, emotions, reactions, and messages. Music, then, is both an expression and reflection of human experience and emotion.

The foundations of modern musical styles were laid down by the first ancient musicians who used wood, rocks, animal skins—and their own bodies—to re-create the sounds of the natural world in which they lived. With their hands, their feet, and their very breath they ignited the passions of listeners and moved them to their feet. The dancing, in turn, had a mesmerizing and hypnotic effect that allowed people to transcend their worldly concerns. Through music they could achieve a level of shared experience that could not be found in other forms of communication. For this reason, music has always been part of religious endeavors, from ancient Egyptian spiritual ceremonies to modern Christian masses. And it has inspired dance movements from kings and queens spinning the minuet to punk rockers slamming together in a mosh pit.

By examining musical genres ranging from Western classical music to rock and roll, readers will find a new understanding of old music and develop an appreciation for new sounds. Books in Lucent's Music Library focus on the music, the musicians, the instruments, and on music's place in cultural history. The songs and artists examined may be easily found in the CD and sheet music collections of local libraries so that readers may study and enjoy the music covered in the books. Informative sidebars, annotated bibliographies, and complete indexes highlight the text in each volume and provide young readers with many opportunities for further discussion and research.

The Culture of Writing in Song

Music and songs have been a central part of human history and culture for thousands of years. Songs help people form communities, understand and describe the world they live in, share their joys and victories, and lament about hard times. Music defines groups, cultures, and even nations, as people use songs to describe themselves, who they are, and what has mattered to them in their lives.

Because it mirrors human experience and development, music changes over time. Some songs and tunes remain popular from one generation to the next, but each generation develops its own musical style that reflects its struggles, accomplishments, and emotions. New songs are written and sung to keep up with social changes; hit songs change as rapidly as any of society's fads. The people who write music strive to create the next popular ditty, even though it may enjoy only fleeting success. Modern songwriters require perseverance, originality, and above all, knowledge of their audience to write songs that will become hits.

The Voices of Generations

Music has always served an important function in human culture. It unites people of a common culture by giving them a particular sound and style they can call their own. People working in mundane or unpleasant jobs over the millennia of human history have done so to song. Armies marching into battle, pirates on raiding ships, slave laborers, and countless others have sung their way through their tasks. Songs for such purposes have always had characteristic rhythms that helped people march or work in tandem. The rhythmic tradition of music is no less important in modern times. A catchy rhythm still makes people sit up and take notice. Modern music depends on rhythm to serve as a background for dance—a practice no less common in modern times than it was in ancient cultures for whom dancing was a common recreational and often spiritual experience.

Music depends on melody as well: the rise and fall of notes and sounds in special (often rhythmic) patterns. Melodies guide musical development in ways rhythm alone cannot. They incite people to sing or hum along. Melodies work their way into listeners' minds and give emotion to music. Classical composers, from the Middle Ages on, have told stories and sagas using melody and rhythm.

Music has long served as a storytelling device. Songs with lyrics have helped people memorialize important events. Countries have national anthems. Folk tales and legends are told through the words of music. Religious holidays are infused with the retelling of important events through the words of song.

Throughout human history, people with a special knack for establishing rhythms, creating emotional melodies, and writing lyrics have chronicled events through music. Songs are stories about humanity, and songwriters have the job of telling these stories in unique ways that make them meaningful for the masses.

History's Storytellers

Music permeates modern culture. The average American between ages eight and eighteen spends an average of two and a half hours a day actively listening to music, according to a 2009 Kaiser Family Foundation study. The average American is exposed to five hours of music every day, much

All people and cultures have music and songs. Songwriters are among the most important storytellers.

of it background music heard in vehicles, homes, workplaces, restaurants, shopping malls, as well as on TV shows, computer programs, and movies.

Although music is a universally human experience, songs are subject to the same shifting trends that affect all of modern society. There are elements of music that sound good together, but joining all of these pieces in creative ways that will be popular with modern listeners is an ongoing challenge. It is difficult to predict what exact songs the public wants to sing or dance to. Making a career out of songwriting is difficult, especially in light of the competition from hundreds of thousands of fellow writers. So while anyone can write songs, not everyone can make hits that shape an important part of the human experience in a lasting way. Still, songwriters remain important storytellers for the current generation, and in today's world, the task has become a profession—sometimes a very lucrative one. Whether they seek a career or just the chance to create musical masterpieces, songwriters are eager to learn what makes music work and use that knowledge to craft memorable songs.

CHAPTER 1

The History of American Pop Music

Every generation sees a new surge of popular songs, or pop music. Popular music often differs from region to region and from generation to generation. Music that is popular at any given time depends largely on the young people of a given generation. Starting as early as the 1950s, teenagers have been the biggest buyers of new music and the biggest predictors of what will become a new musical trend. The Beatles, for example, were an iconic pop music group in the 1960s, but Beatles songs were not necessarily enjoyed by the generations that had grown up in the 1920s, when jazzy dance tunes were all the rage, or in the 1940s, an era of crooners like Bing Crosby. "As in the previous decades, the young people led the trends," says Marcel Danesi, a professor of communication theory. "Young people constituted the force that influenced the mainstream."[1]

In the 1970s, the dance beats of the disco era appealed to the rising youth of a new generation. The 1980s saw big-hair rock bands, and the 1990s experienced a surge in rap music. For today's youth, the music of the 1970s, 1980s, and 1990s are considered oldies, or retro music. Those older styles still influence modern music, but the chart-toppers of yesteryear have been pushed aside for the hits of modern pop music sensations like Beyoncé and Justin Bieber. Even these performers will become oldies as future generations dictate what the next pop music will be.

Songwriters always keep in mind that they write songs for the people who listen to current popular music. Successful songwriters pay close attention to fads and fashions and create songs that will both fit in and stand out among changing musical preferences. The writers of songs that were sung by the Beatles probably would not have much success writing the same kind of tune for today's singers and audiences. "Trends in pop music have defined each era of pop culture," Danesi says, "eventually becoming descriptors of the eras (as in *the jazz era, the rock era, the rap era*, and so on)."[2] Modern songwriters take note of these powerful pop music trends, because they could dictate the success or failure of a song.

The British band the Beatles, seen here in 1963, wrote some of the most enduring pop songs of the late twentieth century. They are now considered oldies or retro, but in their youth they were considered rebels.

The Changing Phenomenon of Pop Music

Although understanding pop music is of critical importance to anyone who wants to write popular modern songs, the idea of pop music is very difficult to define. Its boundaries are always changing. What is popular in any given year will not necessarily be popular the year after. Pop music changes, too, across regions and cultures. In the United States, people in some parts of the country may listen to music that differs from what is popular elsewhere. Music that is popular in cities, for example, sometimes differs from country music,

Tin Pan Alley

By around 1900, commercial music writing and publishing had become concentrated on a single block of Twenty-Eighth Street in New York City. Buildings on the block—which was dubbed Tin Pan Alley—housed the musicians and songwriters who created the tunes that would become the popular music of the day. Music historian Timothy E. Scheurer explains Tin Pan Alley's continuing impact on popular music:

Tin Pan Alley . . . symbolizes not only a type of music produced between 1880 and 1950, but also a style of promotion and production of popular music. . . . It produced . . . some of the country's finest music—music which serves even to this day as a benchmark for popular songwriting throughout the world. It dictated America's musical diet for nearly 70 years, and its influence can still be felt in advertising, movies, radio and any other place where music is produced or used. . . .

Sales of sheet music was the bottom line. People had to buy sheet music to make a song a success. This may seem like an impossibility today, but one must remember that instead of boom boxes and stereos, the turn-of-the-century American had the parlor piano, and moreover, someone in the household more than likely could play. . . . Audience desires, in turn, shaped creativity. Irving Berlin, in many ways the archetypal Tin Pan Alley songsmith, best epitomizes the Alleyman's attitude . . . "I write a song to please the public—and if the public doesn't like it . . . I change it!" Upon that simple philosophy [the popular music] industry was founded and continues to this day.

Timothy E. Scheurer. "The Tin Pan Alley Years (1890–1950): Introduction." *American Popular Music: Readings from the Popular Press Volume I: The Nineteenth Century Tin Pan Alley.* Bowling Green, OH: Bowling Green University Popular Press, 1989.

and popular music in the South is not always the same as the songs blasting out of radios on the West Coast.

Pop music also changes depending on the culture and ethnicity of the listeners. Blacks, whites, and Latinos are cultural groups that tend to have different listening preferences. Songwriters who want to be successful must understand not only generational and geographic differences in music but also the musical genres that appeal to various cultures.

There are loosely three main segments of modern U.S. pop music: country, rock, and rhythm and blues (R&B). All have many subgenres that have become distinct types of music. In addition, all three have historical roots linking them to one another, but each has different sounds and features. Songwriters pair the sound and style of each potential song with the right musical genre in the hope that their songs become modern pop music hits. Understanding each genre is the first step to making that happen.

A Brief History of American Music

The United States is one of the most ethnically diverse nations in the world. Throughout its history, it has absorbed immigrants from all over the globe. Early European settlers also brought hundreds of thousands of African slaves to the United States. The traditions and experiences of these varied ethnic groups have shaped the American experience in countless ways, and they help explain the wide variety of American musical styles.

European settlers in the 1600s brought the musical traditions of their homeland with them to the United States. Their popular music had many of the same features as the classical music of Europe at the time. Religious songs and church hymns were also very common. In the earliest years of the colonial United States, settlers were focused on surviving in the new world. They used music to remember the traditions of home, pray, and survive hard times rather than start any new and inspiring cultural trends.

As the United States grew in size and population, different social classes and geographic regions emerged. Members of

The Birth of the Recording Industry

Until the late nineteenth century, there were two ways to enjoy music—listen to someone else perform it live or create the music oneself. Inventors such as Thomas Edison, who invented the phonograph in 1877, created devices that could record sounds on grooved, rotating plastic discs and other devices that could play these sounds back. For the first time in history, music from a particular singer or band could be recorded. Thousands of copies of the recording could be made, and people everywhere could hear the song by its original singer whenever they chose.

The invention of recording devices changed music forever. Before, popular songs were shared by sheet music and played live by whoever had access to the written songs. Different singers or bands often performed songs in their own way. With records, listeners could hear the original singer or band. Performers became permanently linked to songs, and audiences began to identify songs as belonging to a particu-

Thomas Edison stands in his laboratory in 1920 next to a phonograph, which he invented in 1877.

lar singer. Songwriters still created the songs, but records made the performers into superstars.

the upper class, especially in bigger northern cities like New York and Boston, enjoyed going to orchestra and opera performances like upper classes in Europe had always done. People in the working class, who could not afford trips to fancy musical performances, started making their own kinds of music with the instruments that were available to them. As music historians Kate Van Winkle Keller and John Koegel explain:

The first colonists arrived from and perpetuated a world where the arts were divided. On one side were the cultivated arts of music and dance. . . . On the other side was the music of the people. The laboring, farming, and servant classes had little access to cultivated music. They did not understand it and they did not need it.[3]

Among these working-class musicians, geographic differences took hold. In the Midwest and the South, a rambunctious new style of piano tunes called ragtime became popular. In the South, the introduction of a new musical instrument, the banjo, led to twangy tunes and lyrics that spoke to Southerners' rural way of life. By the late 1800s, the North had its own musical styles, as did the South and the West. Diverse musical styles could also be seen between the wealthy and the poor, as well as city residents and rural folk.

People around the country still sing many of the same church songs and national tunes popular in the late nineteenth century. Songs like "Yankee Doodle" and "Oh My

Before music recordings, songs were distributed as sheet music. The first edition of The Star Spangled Banner—which was a popular song for more than a hundred years before it became the U.S. national anthem—was published in 1814.

The First U.S. Songwriter

Today's professional songwriters can make a lot of money writing and selling popular songs, but the country's first professional songwriter, Stephen Foster, made almost nothing for his efforts. Born in 1826, he lived at a time when most Americans who wanted to enjoy music simply made their own. Foster wrote songs that listeners in those days found catchy, but there would be no recording industry or radio until decades after Foster's death at age thirty-seven. The only way he could make any money for his creative work was by selling copies of the sheet music, which only earned him a small fee. Foster eventually took up the practice of selling his songs to traveling minstrel shows, which moved throughout the country performing for crowds. In this way, Foster's songs migrated throughout the United States. So successful were his tunes that some of them are still well known today, including "Oh! Susanna" and "My Old Kentucky Home." Had Foster lived in modern times, he would likely have been a wealthy songwriter, but despite leaving an enduring legacy in song, he died penniless.

Darling Clementine" have stood the test of time and are still well known today. However, at the turn of the twentieth century, new musical styles began to emerge, reaching far beyond church hymns, patriotic anthems, and ditties about life.

In the 1900s, American society changed in radical ways, and its music reflected this. Slavery had been abolished, and black Americans were free citizens—though not treated fairly in U.S. society. Women fought for the right to vote. The United States weathered two world wars, and in between them, millions found themselves jobless and homeless during the Great Depression.

Technology put its stamp on American life as well. Automobiles closed the distance between rural towns and bigger cities. People went to movie theaters to see films with moving pictures and sound. The phonograph could play recorded tunes on records, and then radio was invented to broadcast recorded music all over the world. Eventually, television made it possible to see performers in action, not just hear their music. "The advent of the phonograph, the sound film [movie], and the radio played an important part in this larger shift in American life," says music professor Timothy D. Taylor. "People were making music less while permitting it to enter their homes with the newer devices."[4]

Technological advances allowed people to buy recordings of popular music rather than make their own music in the streets or on their front porches. Three major musical styles emerged in this record-buying culture: country, rock, and rhythm and blues. The central patterns of modern songs share much with their ancestors. Modern songwriters are, in part, students of musical history, studying the time-honored elements of musical structure even as they try to create something inventive that works within a particular musical style.

The Roots of Country Music

As American music has progressed, many songwriters still turn to the country style of music for its tradition of storytelling and sentimental values. The origins of country music date back to the European folk traditions of minstrel singers in the Middle Ages who traveled from place to place and entertained listeners with stories told through song. In addition to the European folk traditions, country musicians were also inspired by slave spirituals and the blues.

Through the 1800s, many areas of the southern United States remained similar to that of rural Europe. People lived on large pieces of land or in small clusters in the mountains. Before railroads, cars, and telephones were invented, they had little connection to the rest of the country, so they created and shared traditional folk songs about life in their rural setting. Living largely off the land, they respected open spaces and took pride in their rustic lifestyle. They learned to play instruments like the fiddle and the banjo, and these became the background to many tunes played and sung from front porches or at community dances.

In the 1860s, northern and southern states clashed during the Civil War. President Abraham Lincoln abolished the practice of owning slaves, but to people living on plantations in the South, slave ownership was central to their way of life. Eleven southern states attempted to secede from the United States and start their own nation where slavery would be legal. During the Civil War, they fought bitterly for independence from the North. Ultimately, the South lost and remained part of the United States, but their plantation-centered lifestyle was forever changed. For decades afterward, southern music celebrated their country way of life and reflected sentimental memories of the way things used to be.

Modern Country Music

Country music is still known today for its twangy sound. Sentiments of a quieter, simpler lifestyle have never fully vanished from country music and neither have the sounds of string instruments like guitars, fiddles, and banjos. Pride in the country lifestyle remains a common theme as well. "[Country] music has kept itself clean and fairly close to its original themes of family, love, country, and home," says recording artist Cleve Francis. "Country music's reassuring themes are welcomed by many."[5] Hit songs in this genre today include Alan Jackson's "Gone Country," Brooks and Dunn's "You Can't Take the Honky Tonk Out of the Girl," and Brantley Gilbert's "Country Must Be Country Wide," which all reflect the common theme that city life is different than, and often somewhat inferior to, the classic country lifestyle.

For all of its traditions, however, country music has undergone many changes. Modern country songwriters create music with less twang and more of the modern drum beats and guitar sounds common to other musical styles like rock and roll. Today's country songs are increasingly considered *crossovers*, or songs that become popular in multiple genres. Singer-songwriter Taylor Swift and the group Rascal Flatts are two of the many country acts with crossover appeal. Their songs are played almost as frequently on non-country radio stations as on country ones.

Blending country music with other styles has given the genre a wider appeal to young audiences, but fans of traditional country prefer the classic twang of the older country stars such as George Jones, Johnny Cash, Willie Nelson, Loretta Lynn, and Patsy Cline. Country music, while still rooted in country traditions, is in a state of flux. It may be experiencing a shift that will one day mark country as hardly different from other kinds of music in the modern era. To offset this trend and stay true to the history of the genre, many country musicians and songwriters are creating modern songs that echo earlier times and making tunes in styles like bluegrass and Dixieland jazz to balance out the modernized country songs that cross into other genres.

Taylor Swift, a country star with wide crossover appeal, performs at the Academy of Country Music Awards in 2007.

Rocking the Boat

Country music, probably more than any other musical genre, has a history with definite geographic boundaries, even if those boundaries are blurring. Other musical styles have been bound more by generational differences than by geography. Rock music is a significant example. It arose during the latter half of the 1900s, largely because of the invention of a new instrument that created a new way of making songs. If country music has long been defined by banjos and fiddles, rock music has been defined by the electric guitar. In 1937 G.D. Beauchamp and Adolph Rickenbacker invented this new instrument, and jazz musicians of the 1930s and 1940s were the first to incorporate it into their music. However, in the 1950s and 1960s, a new musical form evolved that depended on the electric guitar. This genre became known as rock and roll.

Electric guitars are different from acoustic guitars, because they are connected to an *amplifier* that transmits the signal as a louder sound than an acoustic guitar could ever accomplish. With their amplifiers, electric guitars have a higher volume range, and musicians can sustain notes without fading out the way a strum on an acoustic guitar does. They make much higher pitches and have a greater versatility of tone than acoustic guitars.

With an electric guitar, "guitarists can sustain sounds indefinitely, distort them beyond recognition, and add a host of other effects,"[6] say professional musician Michael Campbell and music professor James Brody. Paired with electric bass guitars for a lower beat and a drum set to help keep the rhythm of a song, electric guitars create a loud, highly energized, sometimes frenzied musical atmosphere. "These instruments were so integral to rock that it is no exaggeration to say that rock music would not have come into being without them,"[7] say Campbell and Brody. Electric instruments are the backbone of rock, which took off in the mid-twentieth century and redefined the music world.

The rock genre broke many musical boundaries. Instrumental music had long been popular, from European classical orchestras to ragtime piano tunes to the brass-band sounds of jazz tunes and swing music in the 1920s. In rock

The development of rock music and songs is directly tied to the invention of the electric guitar and bass.

music, however, the instrumental portions of songs were difficult to write lyrics to, simply because they were so loud. To compete with the sound of a blasting electric guitar, a rock singer had to be equally loud. Some rock musicians chose to shout or even scream the words to their songs.

Lyrics that were written to be screamed often tell an angry story. Rock songs are sometimes rebellious, like Twisted Sister's "We're Not Gonna Take It" or Skid Row's "Youth Gone Wild." Rock singers and songwriters have created countless tender ballads, too, but rock music tends to be louder and have more aggressive lyrics than other musical genres.

The Un-Pop Music

Rock and roll—a mixture of blues, country, and gospel music—originated in the 1950s. It was initially unpopular among the parents and grandparents of teenagers because they mostly thought it was too loud and wild. However, the young generation of the time loved rock and roll, and it has prevailed among every generation since as one of the three main genres of popular music. As with all musical genres, rock and roll branched out in different directions, and in the 1960s, rock—one of its subgenres—took over the U.S. pop charts.

Rock songs from the 1960s and 1970s, performed by artists as diverse as the Beatles, the Rolling Stones, Janis Joplin, and Led Zeppelin, are now considered part of the classic rock genre. Today's teens often listen to modern alternative rock performed by artists like the Foo Fighters, Linkin Park, Pink, and Radiohead. Some rock musicians add synthesizers and keyboards to the mix of electric guitar, bass guitar, and drums to create industrial, Celtic, and punk rock. Heavy metal, marked by bands and artists like Black Sabbath and Marilyn Manson, is generally the loudest of the rock styles and tends to involve the most violent or aggressive lyrics. Other rock subgenres include grunge (performed by bands like Pearl Jam and Nirvana).

In all of its varieties, rock music is ruled by the electric guitar, a strong percussion beat, and singers with voices and lyrics strong enough to keep pace with the powerful instruments of the genre. Rock music is newer than some pop music genres and does not appeal to every listener, but its songwriters and performers have earned a place in the music industry.

Rhythm and Blues

Rhythm and blues encompasses a wide variety of musical styles, instruments, and techniques that trace their roots back to the days of southern plantations and the rich musical traditions slaves brought with them from their African homeland. When slavery came to an end after the Civil War, many newly free African Americans moved away from the southern plantations and into cities. They got jobs, formed communities, and created a new subculture across the country. However, they did not always feel free and happy, and white society often treated them unfairly. They were excluded from many jobs, educational opportunities, and social privileges. Many moved to segregated neighborhoods within bigger cities where they had their own homes, parks, workplaces, restaurants, churches, and traditions—not least of all music. In their various communities at the turn of the twentieth century, African Americans were making music like the country had never heard before.

Much early African American music took the form of the blues. The lyrics of blues songs originally spoke of the hard and hopeless life of slavery, but as free African

Topping the Charts

Billboard is an international magazine reporting on the music industry. It was founded in 1894 as a weekly publication reporting on live entertainment like circuses and carnivals. In the 1930s, when jukeboxes became popular, *Billboard* began reporting on popular songs. It calculated its first music popularity chart in 1940. By 1958, *Billboard* consolidated its first Top-100 chart for music singles popular on the radio and in sales. *Billboard* now charts the top two hundred songs every week, ranking their popularity based on how often they are played on radio stations, how many hard copies are sold, and how many times the song is downloaded from a digital vendor like iTunes. *Billboard* ranks various music genres, including pop, dance/club, hip hop, R&B, rap, rock, alternative, country, and Latin, and it also combines all the categories to rank the top two hundred.

Billboard maintains records for the top position any song has received in the past several decades, as well as how long it stayed on the charts. For songwriters, having one of their songs land high on the *Billboard* rankings is a mark of success.

A cover of Billboard *magazine from 2011 features singer-songwriter Alyssa Rubino.*

Americans tried to fit in with the white culture, they found that things still were not easy. They continued to sing the blues as a way to share their social frustrations. "If there is any common element in debates about the roots of the blues, it is that they came into being as an expression of African American experience," says music studies professor Philip V. Bohlman. "Different regions—the Southeast, the Southwest, the Mississippi Delta—lay claim to their own blues histories."[8] By the early 1900s, the musical style was catching on everywhere, from the country to big cities such as Chicago and Detroit.

African American blues evolved into jazz, a style of music that paired brass instruments like the trumpet and the saxophone. Jazz could be smooth and relaxing or peppy and invigorating. People could dance to it and sing along with it. It set new trends as a musical form and became increasingly popular in the early 1900s, especially with the invention of records that allowed singers and bands to put their music into a physical form. "Although music resembling jazz had existed in various forms prior to the start of the twentieth century, the genre began to forge its true identity around 1910," says musician biographer David Dicaire. "But in order for the new style to truly catch on in the public's mind, widespread popularity had to be established. The obvious answer was the technology of recording."[9]

Motown and Soul

By the 1920s, blacks and whites alike enjoyed listening to blues and jazz tunes. These two musical styles became part of almost every other musical movement in the United States. They also evolved into other forms of music, such as rhythm and blues and soul, which eventually found their way into mainstream America and began topping music charts.

Motown—with groups such as the Temptations (back row) and the Supremes (front)—defined 1960s American pop music.

Black communities had strong churches and choirs, and black religious music, known as gospel, led to the emergence of soul music in the 1950s. Soul had secular themes, but was driven by gospel-like musical devices. Artists like Ray Charles, James Brown, and Sam Cooke created powerful hit songs that crossed cultural boundaries. The tradition of black gospel music has helped shape the careers of many African American singers ever since. In the 1980s, for example, Whitney Houston became one of the country's biggest pop stars, and much of her musical training came from participating in her community church's choir.

Rhythm and blues emerged in the 1940s, but soared to new heights in the 1960s with the popularity of Motown Records in Detroit, Michigan. Motown launched the careers of superstars like Smokey Robinson, the Temptations, Diana Ross and the Supremes, the Jackson 5, and Stevie Wonder. Memorable melodies, group harmonies, and toe-tapping beats marked the Motown sound, and Americans could not get enough of it. "Motown became mass culture," says history professor Matthew C. Whitaker. "Public demand to see The Supremes or The Temptations in concert persuaded promoters to book Motown groups in much larger venues."[10] The popularity of rhythm and blues helped black musicians overcome the belief that their music could never become mainstream.

R&B Gets Funky

In the 1970s, some R&B songwriters and performers took the focus off of melody and harmony and placed it on rhythm. The result was a new, dance-ready musical style called funk, with songs like Rick James's "Super Freak" and the Commodores' "Brick House" topping R&B charts. Disco music similarly put a focus on a dance-floor rhythm. Through the 1980s, R&B artists Michael Jackson and Whitney Houston dominated American pop music. And in the 1990s, another R&B form arose that added a new dimension to American music—rap.

Based on fast-talking verbal games that had long been popular in African American communities, rap music

James Brown (right)—a rhythm-and-blues star and the originator of the danceable style called funk—teaches dance moves to Johnny Carson on the latter's late night talk show in 1967.

was street music with a catchy beat, tongue-twisting lyrics, and often, no musical instruments to accompany it at all. "Groups of kids had only to gather on a neighborhood street, using nothing but their voices to make music that would, eventually, develop worldwide appeal,"[11] says musicology professor Albin J. Zak III. In 1979 a group called the Sugarhill Gang produced "Rapper's Delight," the first hit single in this R&B subgenre. By the 1990s, rap music had a huge following and was a major sector of the American music scene. Today, rap music is as popular with white audiences as black ones.

The Melting Pot of Modern Music

Along with today's dance tunes and popular radio ballads, R&B largely dominates the pop music scene—so much so that pop and R&B often seem like one and the same genre. Country and rock songs borrow elements from the long, varied creative history of R&B music, from blues to jazz, soul, and rap. Songwriters who aspire to create hit music have a wide variety of musical styles at their disposal. Today more than ever, songs cross genres, sometimes making songwriting a challenging task, because there are so many styles and techniques from which to choose. American music, like U.S. society as a whole, has become a melting pot of different cultural influences, styles, and backgrounds. Songwriters strive to choose a blend of elements in the hope of achieving a boundary-crossing, nationwide hit.

CHAPTER 2

Melody, Harmony, and Rhythm

People are surrounded by music almost everywhere they go. It serves as a backdrop for everyday public adventures, from theme parks to department stores to restaurants and elevator rides. It is a constant presence in all forms of entertainment, even when people do not actively seek it. Music shows up in stage performances, movies, television shows, commercials, and even during phone calls if the listener is put on hold. It has the power to evoke particular moods and feelings, such as calmness or cheer in a shopping mall and sadness or dread in a movie. It may be the most emotional of any human art form, and when created well, it is certainly one of the most powerful.

Inventors of new music need an innate understanding of what musical elements will sound good together and how these elements will be performed best. Certain styles of songs sound better on a piano, for example. Others may require a fiddle, a saxophone, or an electric guitar. Percussion instruments help establish the beat or rhythm of the song. Many elements must work together in new and creative ways if a song is to appeal to listeners, because even people with no formal training in music naturally seem to know which noises sound good together and which do not.

Composers of classical music have always been considered true musical artists for their ability to piece together all

The Mood of a Song

Melodies are arrangements of notes. When played in a certain order, notes create scales. When multiple notes are played together, they create chords. Depending on the root note, or starting note of a scale, the other notes relative to it are considered major or minor. Whether a melody and its related harmony are created with mostly major or minor notes affects the mood of the song. Major notes typically create melodies that sound strong and happy. Minor notes tend to evoke feelings of sadness or restlessness. Factors like the tempo, or speed, of a melody also help determine whether it is cheery or sad, but even very young children can pick up on the fact that songs with minor harmonies tend to sound gloomy.

This is not to say that all minor-key songs are glum or that upbeat songs avoid minor keys. In fact, most modern hit songs use a combination of major and minor keys, which reflects the fact that many songs tell stories with complicated themes and feelings. Songwriters must be aware, however, of the way minor and major keys can affect a listener's mood, so their song's message comes across the way they intend.

the parts of an orchestra into a unified symphony of sound. Classical music is still a very important genre and is far more complex than most modern pop music. However, the creators of new tunes in genres like pop, rock, country, and R&B also possess an innate understanding of how the various elements of music go together. When they compose their music, they decide on a song's purpose, mood, and meaning. They pair together a melody and a rhythm that will help the song achieve its purpose, and they put these pieces together in ways that will capture the listener's imagination and send the message they want the song to convey. It is a challenging task but one that can have big rewards for the songwriter if his or her tune catches the interest of listeners.

Melody Is a Song's Skeleton

Most songs have various layers, often played by multiple instruments all working together at the same time. These layers can be dissected one at a time to examine what is happening in the song. As the different layers are peeled away, one of the layers that is left could be called the skeleton of the song, or its most basic recognizable part. This is the song's melody. It is the part of the song that a listener can hum and can be played on a piano with just one finger. "The melody is usually the most memorable aspect of a song, the one the listener remembers and is able to perform,"[12] says songwriter and songwriting instructor Jack Perricone.

Melodies can be dissected even further, into individual notes. A note is one specific sound, and there are seven natural notes: A, B, C, D, E, F, and G. Each of these differs from the others in *pitch*, or how high or low the note sounds. On a piano, these seven natural notes are the white keys, and the five black keys in between are the sharp and flat notes. Pianos have more than seven white keys and five black keys, so eventually, playing each note in order beginning with an A, the player will come back to A in a higher pitch. The high-pitched A and the low-pitched A are still the same note. They have the same sound, or tone, just with a different degree of sounding low and deep or high and shrill.

Each of the seven natural notes, or white piano keys, can be played in order to create a scale, which is like taking musical steps up or down the piano keys. The natural notes, played in order, create the common scales, C major and A minor. The C major scale moves from the C note through all the other notes to end up at the next higher C note on the piano. It also comes back down again, from the high C to the lower C.

To make melodies more interesting, there are also sharp and flat notes, or notes that sit between the seven natural notes. These in-between notes are the black keys on a piano. They are known as sharp versions of the natural note to their immediate left on the piano, or as flat versions of the natural note to their immediate right. These notes are

Musical notes from the same scale are combined to create a melody.

half steps that fit in between the sounds of the natural notes. (Two pairs of natural notes, B–C and E–F, do not have a half-step flat or sharp note that fits between them, so each pair of white keys appears together on a piano with no black key in between.)

Melodies are made by stringing together individual notes into a particular sequence. The notes can skip out of order in a melody: C might jump to F, for example, skipping over D and E. A melody can use any combination of notes. It can start at a low pitch and rise to a higher pitch, or start at a high pitch and drop to a lower one. The notes of a melody can also last for different amounts of time. Some notes can be short, letting the melody move quickly to a new note. Other notes can be held for a long time.

Whatever series of notes is chosen to create a melody, it should have emotion and meaning behind it. "If you only use your rational mind in composing a song," Perricone says, "you will most likely have an undesirable result—a dry, unmoving group of notes, logically organized, but emotionally barren."[13] On the other hand, a meaningful mix of high notes and low notes as well as long notes and short ones creates the melody that determines the dramatic structure—and possibly the future success—of a song.

Chords Are a Song's Muscle

Without a melody, or the part that a person can hum along with, a pop song would make little sense. Creating the melody, therefore, is often the starting point of a new song. Even after songwriters have come up with a catchy melody, however, their song is far from complete. A person can usually hum a song so that listeners can tell what tune it is, but rarely can anyone hum every layer of a popular song unless it is something like "Happy Birthday to You," which is a simple melody with no embellishments.

The melody creates the musical structure of a song, but by itself, it is not usually very remarkable. It may even be similar to the melodies of other songs because there are only twelve different musical notes to work with in the common Western musical scale, including flats and sharps. Millions of melodies have already been written using these exact same notes, and there are only so many different ways to put them together. To create a catchy, mesmerizing, or magical song, the melody requires additional sounds that help support the notes and give them interest, meaning, and originality.

The parts of a song that support the melody make up its harmony. Harmony is created by using chords, individual notes, or groups of notes (usually three or more) played at the same time to create a unique sound that complements the melody. The harmonic aspects of a song are often played in a lower key than the melody, and for this reason they are sometimes called the bass line, or the low-pitched harmonic

All Roads Lead Back Home

Most songs in modern popular music have what is known as a *home note*. Usually the first note heard in the song, it sets up the main sound of the song. The melody will wander away to other notes but usually comes back to the home note often. Listeners may not be aware of exactly what a home note is, at least not consciously, but once they hear the home note of a song, they listen for the melody to return to that note again. The longer it takes for the song to revisit its home note, the more listeners want to hear it and the more tension the song will create. Returning to the home note, on the other hand, often signifies the end of the song.

Ending on the home note is usually the most pleasing way to wrap up a tune. Some songs end on other notes, but these usually leave listeners feeling as if the song has no real resolution or end. For the most part, however, songwriters try to please audiences by ending songs where they started, on the home note.

notes of song. The harmony is connected to the melody like the body's muscles are connected to bones. "Concentrating on the bass might not be easy at first," says music professor Craig M. Wright. "Most of us have always thought that listening to music means listening to the melody. . . . But the bass is next in importance, and it rules supreme in a sort of subterranean world."[14]

Both the bass line and the melody work together to make the entire song sound richer. Rarely do chords stand out in contrast to the melody. Instead, they tend to create a background for the melody—the way backup singers often add to a lead singer's performance but rarely overtake the lead singer's strength in a song. In the same way, a song's melody is what listeners notice, remember, and sing, but the chords can take a boring melody and make it sound rich and complete.

Anatomy of a Chord

Chords are not just any group of notes played together at once. Some notes sound good together and create a harmony. Other notes clash when played together at the same time. If several adjoining piano keys are all pressed down at once, the sound is usually not pleasing to the ear. Chords, on the other hand, are pleasing to listen to, because they consist of carefully selected notes, usually with one or more spaces between them.

Guitars and pianos are two instruments that can play simultaneous notes and thus can produce chords. Musicians who learn to play these instruments practice playing many different chords whose notes fit well together. The more

Jazz singer-songwriter Esperanza Spalding accompanies herself on a standup bass during a TV performance in 2011. The bass line is an essential harmonic component of a song that gives it depth and structure.

chords a songwriter knows, the more original songs he or she can create. Just as chords consist of specific notes that sound good when played together, a particular note in a song's melody will sound good when played with certain chords but not with others. Usually, any particular note in the melody (such as C) is paired with a chord that also has that note in it. Because there are many chords that have the C note in them, songwriters who know a lot of chords can try out different options that are harmonious with the melody to determine which sounds the best.

Although they are carefully chosen, chords and harmony remain in the background of a song. They are not the part that average listeners remember most about a tune. In fact, many modern hit songs use only three or four chords. "In popular music, sensing when the harmony changes can be easier because it is more common for a succession of chord changes to repeat over and over again in exactly the same

A man plays a chord—several harmonious notes played at the same time—on a Gibson Les Paul guitar.

pattern,"[15] Wright says. Nevertheless, the chords and harmony have a very important role in popular music. They give mood to a song, because people tend to perceive some chords as happy and uplifting and others as sad. Chords are also one of the first things a listener might hear in the song, because they may be used in a song's introduction before the melody starts.

Choosing from the wide variety of possible chords can help make songs sound very different from other tunes. All music uses variations and harmonies of the same twelve notes, but the almost endless possibilities of melodic notes and chords help songwriters create new music with original layers of sound.

Rhythm Is a Song's Heartbeat

Melody and harmony are important elements of songs, but they are rarely the only tools songwriters use. Just as chords give depth and interest to a melody, rhythm adds depth to the song as a whole. Rhythm is to music what the heart is to the body. It gives a regular, steady beat to a song and nudges it along from start to finish.

Rhythm is a pattern of sounds that repeats itself. A bouncing ball has rhythm, as does a ticking clock. In music, though, rhythms tend to be complex and involve many different types of sounds. A melody is the part of a song that listeners can hum, but rhythm is the part to which they can tap their feet, nod their heads, or dance. A song's rhythm can be fast or slow, but just as with melodies and chords, a rhythm that is too repetitive can get boring. A song's rhythm usually changes pace, or tempo, at different points in a song, perhaps increasing as the melody reaches its highest and most significant notes and slowing down during more thoughtful or sad sections of the melody. Whatever its tempo, however, the rhythm drives the song steadily toward its end. "Think of rhythm as the engine that moves the music forward and gives it the feeling of always going somewhere,"[16] says composer William Duckworth.

Rhythm is found in all layers of a song. The melody, with its combination of short and long notes, creates rhythm on

Rhythm is the part of the music you can move your body to.

its own. The chords of a song do, too. They might change quickly or stay the same for one or more notes, and this helps establish a certain rhythm. "All music has a rhythmic component," Duckworth says. "All of us can feel it; it's one of the musical elements we respond to first."[17]

In modern popular music, listeners usually expect rhythm to be a very strong component of the song. Often, rhythm is the first thing they hear, even before the chords or the melody. Depending on the type of song, the rhythm can be even more important than the melody. This was a trend that was prevalent in disco and funk music of the 1970s. In these genres, a song's beat and rhythm made it distinct, catchy, popular, and fun to dance to. The same is true for pop music of today, especially music that is intended for dancing. Because modern listeners demand it, songwriters make sure a song's beat is as well established as its melody and harmony.

Making a Good Beat

Some songs become almost instantly popular and stay that way for a long time; such songs are often said to have a good beat. Defining a *good* beat can be difficult. It is easier to define what a beat is in general. Songs are divided into measures—segments defined by the repeated pattern of equally spaced beat sounds (which may be easier to think of as toe taps). Some songs have only two major beats, or toe taps, per measure. Counted out as *one* two, *one* two, this is sometimes known as a foxtrot beat and was popular in music of the 1920s. Some songs, especially in classical music, have three beats per measure, a rhythmic style known as a waltz and counted out as *one* two three, *one* two three.

In the 1930s, swing music became popular, and it had four beats per measure. From the 1950s to the 1960s, songwriters and performers created a new kind of music generally with a four-beat measure: rock and roll. What set rock-and-roll songs apart from other four-beat styles was the presence of a backbeat, or an emphasis on the second and fourth beat of every measure. The emphasis is usually created by a tinny drum sound on those alternating beats, perhaps from a snare drum or a cymbal. If the main beats are played with a deeper drum sound, the differently pitched drum sound will accent beats two and four in every measure, and the rhythm can be counted out as one *two* one *two*. A good example of an early rock song with a backbeat is Bill Haley's "Rock Around the Clock" from 1955. The backbeat-heavy rhythm style has become one of the defining features of rock music.

The four-beat rhythm with a backbeat on every second and fourth sound has become one of the most popular and common rhythm structures in pop music today. It is not used just in rock music but spans the genres, showing up in ballads, dance hits, and rap tunes. The backbeat is one of the things listeners might unconsciously search for to determine whether a song has that hard-to-define *good* beat.

Listeners also notice syncopation, which is something unexpected that is added to a song, often to its rhythm, to create interest. In a four-beat measure, a steady drum beat pounding out *one, two, three, four* for the whole song could quickly get monotonous, the same way a melody of the same notes sung in the same four-beat rhythm, *la, la, la, la,* would. Syncopation uses added percussion sounds within the typical four-beat structure, along with extra, unexpected notes in the melody or chords in the harmony to give interest to a song. "Syncopation is a rhythm or accent that does not line up in an expected way with the beat or other regular rhythm,"[18] say Michael Campbell and James Brody.

The reason syncopation works is because listeners like to be surprised. Rhythm, melody, and harmony are generally repeated throughout a song, which builds up listeners' expectations to hear the same thing again. When there is a syncopation—an unexpected change—it catches a listener's attention. Maroon 5's 2011 hit "Moves Like Jagger," for example, has rhythmic shifts, and these catchy parts may become a person's favorite part of a song. "The tension created by the interplay between the regular rhythms and the rhythms that fall off the beat creates much of the rhythmic interest of the song," say Campbell and Brody. "More than any other aspect of the rhythm, it is what gives the song a 'good beat.'"[19]

Most listeners immediately perk up their ears when the beat of an entire song has an unusual variation on a standard four-beat rhythm. Even if they do not know exactly why they like it, they will generally think that a song with a syncopated rhythm has a great beat.

Creating the Beat

With or without syncopation, a song's rhythm is its heartbeat and lifeline. In almost all popular music today, regardless of genre, the beat is well defined throughout the song, usually with drums. In fact, drums tapping out the rhythm are usually one of the first sounds, if not the very first, that a listener hears. For songwriters, setting up the initial beat is important because it tells listeners what to expect from the song, such as its tempo, or the number of beats (toe taps) per minute of the song. Within the first few beats, the listener will know from the tempo what kind of song

Adam Levine of the band Maroon 5 co-wrote their hit song "Moves Like Jagger," which features a synco-pated guitar riff.

to expect: perhaps a dance tune with a tempo of about 120 beats per minute (bpm) that dancers can keep up with, a rock song with a tempo of 140 to 160 bpm, or a fast-paced, highly energized song with about 180 bpm.

The actual sounds used to create the rhythm and tempo also give the listener clues about what to expect from the song. Drum sets, which are commonly used in rock songs, can create various sounds, from a deep-sounding bass drum for a steady four-beat rhythm to a higher-pitched snare drum for the backbeat. In addition, drum sets can add unusual or unexpected percussion sounds to the steady drone of the time-keeping bass and the backbeat noise of the snare drum. The crash of cymbals can create an exciting emphasis in a song. The more soulful sound of hand-beaten drums like bongos or congas can give music a Latin sound, and djembe drums (pronounced JEM-bay) can help give music an African mood.

Drums, while popular, are not the only instruments that can create a song's rhythm. Much modern pop music, especially rock, uses an electric bass guitar, a guitar with a deep, low sound that often creates the underlying beats that support the common four-beat structure in a song. Some musical styles accomplish beat and rhythm without any musical instruments at all. Hip-hop music, for example, was first created on the streets of inner cities by musicians who used no instruments. Their only form of percussion was sound effects they created with their mouths, throats, and hands, a musical talent known as beatboxing. "The voice is a rhythm instrument as well as a melodic one, capable of emphasizing beats as if it were a set of drums,"[20] says music critic and writer Frank Kogan. Professional beatboxers are so good at their craft that it is nearly impossible to tell their songs use no musical instruments of any kind. Beatboxing is still popular today and provides a background for the music of

Doug E. Fresh (left)—the self-proclaimed first human beatbox—performs with Will Smith in 2011.

many rap artists, taking the place of traditional drums, bass guitars, or other instruments normally used to create the beat of a song. "Rap music centers on the human voice,"[21] Kogan says.

Whatever the method for creating rhythm, it is a part of every song. It gives dimension to the melody and the harmonies, and it drives the song toward its conclusion. Rhythm also establishes the mood of a song—such as happy, angry, or sad—and can give it important cultural touches such as a Caribbean reggae beat.

Rhythm, like harmony, may not be the part of a song to which listeners hum or sing along, but it is certainly the part to which they nod their heads, tap their feet, or dance. It is one of the important layers of any song, and songwriters must make sure the rhythm works together with the song's harmony and melody to create a finished product that catches listeners' attention, lulls them in with patterns, and surprises them from time to time with syncopation before drawing to a close.

Putting It All on Paper

The ability to invent and combine different elements of songs to create a polished whole is part of a songwriter's talent. A songwriter experiments with numerous elements as he or she imagines how the finished song will sound. The songwriter starts with a melody as the skeleton of the song and then fleshes it out with chords and rhythm. These musical elements must work together to make a song stand out and hopefully become a hit. Once a songwriter fits all the song's pieces together, he or she records the song and has to communicate his or her ideas to other musicians who will be able to perform the song.

One way songwriters convey their ideas to others is by using sheet music. Songs are written down on five-line staff paper, which shows the notes of the melody and how long or short each melodic note is. Sheet music also shows the chords the songwriter has come up with and which ones are to be played during which part of the melody. It also shows a song's rhythm, because the five-line segments (staffs) are

All of the composition's components— melody, chords, and rhythm—come together on sheet music.

divided into *measures,* or lengths with a certain number of major beats, usually four per measure. Sheet music tells whether certain notes of the melody are to be clipped short, drawn out, or strung together in a smooth rise or fall of pitch, as well as which notes should be played loudly and which should be soft. Sheet music is written in a special language that puts the story of a song from the songwriter's imagination into a visual form that other musicians can read and copy. It is basically the written language of music and can be a very effective way to communicate musical ideas back and forth, especially in genres like classical music, in which songs are very complex.

Accurately writing down a song into musical notation is a way to get the story from the songwriter's imagination into the minds of other musicians. "If a song is going to be recorded by an artist for commercial release, it is a good idea to supply the producer with a full lead sheet," or sheet music that shows the song's melody, harmony, and lyrics, says songwriter and music instructor Elizabeth C. Axford. "Having strong ideas initially," she says, "will best help to influence the outcome of the final production."[22]

Musicians also want to sing the song, of course, and at this point, songwriters still have something important to do

Film Scores: Music and Songs for Movies

Filmmakers use music in most mainstream movies to create specific moods in different scenes. Music can support the action on screen to evoke the desired mood from the audience—sadness, amusement, anxiety, or relief, for example. Most moviegoers are usually unaware of the *film score*—a musical composition written specifically for a movie—or of the effects it may have on them. Because film scores are meant to complement the movie's action and dialogue, not distract from it, most scores have no lyrics.

Music and songs are so important in movies that there are Academy Awards specifically devoted to their creators. Although not all songs from movies become independently famous, songwriters can build successful careers writing for films. Major movie studios often pay more than a hundred thousand dollars per project to composers and songwriters.

Singer-songwriter Randy Newman (center) is perhaps best known as a film composer. Among his acclaimed works are the score and songs for several Pixar films including the Toy Story *trilogy.*

for the song to be complete—they have to write the actual words that go along with the great melody, harmony, and rhythm they have thus far created. These words are the lyrics, and because they transform a tune into something that can actually be sung with a human voice, they are often as important as the melody, harmony, and rhythm of a song combined.

CHAPTER 3

All in the Words

Melody, harmony, and rhythm are defining parts of a song, and in musical genres like orchestral music and jazz, these may be all a song needs. In most modern popular music, however, listeners want to hear more than an instrumental piece of music. They actually want to sing along, and for this, songs need words. A song's job is to tell a story of some kind, and the words of a song, called its lyrics, help it to do so. Lyrics also serve the important function of making a song memorable in a way that melody and rhythm often cannot. Listeners may like a song because they can dance to its beat, but they usually love a song they can sing along with. Listeners tend to identify with lyrics most in a song.

Many songwriters begin crafting a new song by first writing out the words and then coming up with a melody to match them. Other songwriters work in pairs, with one person writing melodies and harmonies and the other writing the words of the song. Lyrics seldom make a bad song good, but the right lyrics can make a good song great.

Songs Tell Stories

People have always told stories through songs. Traveling minstrels of the Middle Ages wandered among villages

In some songwriting teams, one person focuses on the music and the other on the words.

and towns telling stories of important people and events through song. Folk tales in many cultures, including that of early Americans, were often set to song to make them easier to share and remember. Throughout human history, musical lyrics have been ways to share news and pass cultural beliefs and stories to future generations. Today, most songs still resemble short stories of some kind. They have characters, and the characters usually have a problem to work out or a goal to meet by the end of the song. "Song lyrics, like television programs, create a fantasy world in which characters act, plots unfold, and lessons become clear,"[23] says media studies professor Gary Burns.

Unsung Heroes

When singers perform songs, they often do it with such passion that listeners mistakenly believe the performers are singing about their own lives and experiences and that the song ideas came from them. In the case of some singer-songwriters, this might be true, but many artists perform songs written by someone else. Furthermore, most songwriters try to create a musical story that any good singer could tell.

Unfortunately for songwriters, audiences of listeners associate songs with performers so strongly that they never spend much time thinking someone else actually *wrote* the song. Some hits by Rihanna, Britney Spears, and Mariah Carey have been written by men, for example, even though the songs are in first person, and it sounds like the performers are singing about their own ex-

periences. What listeners might come to think of as a "Rihanna" song may actually owe its existence to someone else entirely, even though she was the one who brought the song to life with her voice. Songwriters rarely enjoy the same fanfare as the singers who get famous from their songs.

Singer-songwriter The-Dream (right) has co-written many songs performed by Rihanna (left).

The most important character in a song is usually the narrator, the one who tells the story. Song lyrics may be written in first person, where the narrator refers to himself or herself as *I* or *we*. Most love songs use first-person lyrics because their main character is usually someone who has fallen in love or whose heart has been broken and wants to tell about the experience. First person is also used to show that the narrator has learned an important and personal lesson about life. Songs written in first person tend to feel intimate. Listeners may imagine themselves as the narrator and often feel that the song captures their own feelings, dreams, or fears. Song lyrics written in first person can be so convincing that listeners think the singer, perhaps someone like Adele, is telling about her own feelings and experiences—and, in most of Adele's self-written songs, she actually is.

Other song lyrics are written in second person, meaning that the narrator is talking to someone in particular or to all listeners in general. Songs written in second person often use the word *you*. When a song is written in second person, the narrator's goal is often to convince listeners to take action and do something, such as take better care of the planet or be kind to other people. Joni Mitchell's 1970 hit "Big Yellow Taxi," for example, addresses listeners directly when it asks them to consider the effects of destroying nature for modern conveniences. Some songs' lyrics mix first and second person. This often happens if the narrator is addressing a particular person about his or her feelings, such as when Taylor Swift, in her 2010 song "Mean," directly addresses people who have bullied her.

Joni Mitchell performs at a 1995 music festival. Her well-crafted songs expertly employ character and voice.

The third option is for a song to be written in third person, meaning that the narrator is telling the story of other people. In third-person song lyrics, the narrator uses words like *he*, *she*, and *they* to tell the story. In such song lyrics, the narrator usually is not taking part in what is happening but observing someone else and telling listeners about it. Unlike songs written solely in first person, which are often snapshots of the narrator's feelings about something, songs written in third person tend to seem more like actual stories. Listeners try to picture what the characters look like, where they are, and what they are doing, so such song lyrics need details about their characters and their setting. Suzanne Vega's 1981 hit "Tom's Diner" is a song with a strong setting and visible characters, as are many country hits that double as stories, like "The Gambler" (1978), written by Don Schlitz and performed by Kenny Rogers or "Live Like You Were Dying" (2004), written by Tim Nichols and Craig Wiseman and performed by Tim McGraw.

Choosing the right point of view in the lyrics of a song is one of a songwriter's main tasks. "The point of view and perspective of the singer is very important," says social psychologist Robert Krout, "and may be the first aspect [of the song] to consider."[24] The same story can be told in first, second, or third person with very different results. First-person songs are like being inside the speaker's head, whereas third-person songs are like sitting next to the speaker looking around a room at what he or she sees. Songs written entirely in second person may seem bossy, like they are telling listeners what to do. Choosing the right person for a song depends largely on what the characters' goals will be, because songs, like any good story, show what characters want and whether or not they get it.

Structuring the Story

Whether a song's lyrics tell a story in first, second, or third person, listeners expect the character to do something or change somehow during the song. Songwriters have a lot to accomplish in very little time and space. "A song must have a story with a beginning, a middle, and an end,"[25] says songwriter Pamela Phillips Oland. Writing good lyrics requires songwriters to narrow down exactly what it is that they want to say about their characters and then give those characters a chance to learn something by the end of the story.

When creating lyrics, songwriters follow certain patterns that go along with the melody of a song. In most songs, verses alternate with a chorus, which tends to have a different melody and different lyrics than the verses. The chorus is repeated every time it appears in the song. A popular song arrangement has three verses, each followed by a repetition of the chorus. The chorus contains the main point the songwriter is trying to get across. The verses develop the story,

Writing Songs Any Artist Can Sing

To sell their music to artists, songwriters often try to make their melodies and lyrics stand out. They must be careful, however, because getting too creative or complicated can make a song hard to sing. If a tune has a large range in pitch, for example, meaning it has both very low and very high notes, it may be hard to find performers who can sing it. Although such songs could become big hits, publishers sometimes turn them down because they do not have a singer in mind who can handle the complex melodies.

Lyrics, too, can limit the number of potential buyers for a song. In particular, if the narrator of the song is distinctly male or female, such as in a song about fatherhood or motherhood, the song will be limited to performers of just one gender. This can cut the number of singers potentially interested in a songwriter's tune in half. New songwriters, especially, must be careful to write songs whose lyrics and melodies could be sung by almost any musician. If not, their songs run the risk of not being bought at all.

so that the character or characters must change a little or learn something new in each verse. The chorus repeatedly reminds listeners of the main idea of the song. "Write lyrics that clearly lead your listeners to one idea," says songwriter Jason Blume. "This idea will be encapsulated by your title and/or chorus."[26]

The structure of most songs follows some kind of verse-chorus-verse repetition. The verses set up the story and show the character facing a problem or dilemma of some kind, as well as how he or she reacts to it during the course of the song. The chorus drives home the main idea of the story. Choruses usually stand out because they are repeated during the song. Many people find they can sing along with the chorus of a new song after hearing it just one time, which helps a song deliver the message the songwriter is trying to tell.

The Relationship Between Songwriting and Poetry

When song lyrics are written out, they often look like a poem. Song lyrics share many similarities to poems. The verses and choruses can be separated into sections that look like a poem's stanzas, or groups of lines. Most songs are also poem-like in that many use rhyme, especially at the end of a *melodic phrase* (a group of notes, put to a particular rhythm, that go along with a line of lyrics in the song). Rhyme ties the lyrics of a song together, and listeners anticipate rhyming words because these are pleasing to hear and help set up predictable verses and choruses.

When done well, rhyme can enhance a song and make it memorable. However, too much rhyme or the wrong kind of rhyme can also ruin a song. Songwriters cannot choose lyrics that do not fit well into the song's story just to make a rhyme. The word *loose* may rhyme with *goose*, for example, but that does not mean the words make sense together in the same song. Because song lyrics tell stories in such a short amount of space, every word has to be the perfect word to help tell the story—and must rhyme, if necessary, in the process. This is one of the challenges of writing great

Jingle Tunes

Songwriters do more than just write hit songs. There is demand for music in other fields, too, especially advertising. Companies often use advertising agencies to create television or radio commercials. These are often centered on a short, catchy, memorable tune—an advertising jingle.

Writing good jingles has a lot in common with any kind of songwriting in that jingles set lyrics to interesting melodies. Instead of telling a story, though, these lyrics describe a product in a way that makes people remember it. Jingles are very short, often just a few words of lyrics set to a simple melody. The entire jingle serves as the hook. The best ones stick immediately in listeners' heads. Ideally, listeners will come away singing the jingle (and thus will remember the name of the product). Although jingles can be annoying, they are also effective. Anyone who spells out Oscar Mayer's "B-O-L-O-G-N-A" or is told to "break me off a piece of that Kit Kat Bar" is almost certain to remember the product. Songwriters who create jingles have a special form of genius. Once heard, a jingle may stick with listeners for a lifetime.

song lyrics. Rhymes are integral to most songs, but if they are too obvious or predictable, a song might end up sounding childish, silly, or too poetic to be realistic. "If you twist your words around just to get a rhyme, you've immediately turned your song into a poem,"[27] Oland says.

Fortunately, songwriters, like poets, do not always have to use words that rhyme exactly. They can choose words with similar long vowel sounds that give much the same effect as direct rhymes in a song. For example, ending two lines of lyrics with the words *night* and *sigh* has almost the same sound effect as choosing directly rhyming words like *night* and *plight*, but *sigh* is a more common word and may fit much better in the lyrics and the story. A lyric that pairs *plight* with *night* just for the sake of a rhyme risks sounding forced and unnatural, much the same way that a poem may sound forced if it uses awkward words just because they rhyme with each other.

The similarities between lyrics and poetry do not stop at rhymes. Song lyrics use many poetic devices to tell stories. Lyrics might use imagery, for example, to help a listener picture what the song is about. Common types of imagery are comparisons between two unrelated things that make the listener see them differently. Similes are such comparisons that use the words *like* or *as*. An example would be Nelly Furtado's "I'm Like a Bird," released in 2000. The song is about how the main character sees herself as a flighty, nervous, and wandering sort of person, characteristics normally associated with birds. Other comparisons, called metaphors, show how two things are similar without using the words *like* or *as*. An example of a song with metaphors is Rascal Flatts's 2006 version of "Life Is a Highway." The song draws similarities between the journey through life and the experience of driving down a road.

Not all songs use similes and metaphors, and not all song lyrics rhyme either. The most important thing about writing lyrics is to tell a story successfully within the time frame of the song. Successful songwriters choose from a variety of techniques to make their point effectively and help the listener visualize what is happening in the song's story. Like poems, songs often convey complicated ideas and feelings using few words, but unlike poems, the words of songs must fit into melodies and specific time frames, and songs also must be fairly easy for listeners to understand. "Successful lyrics have to compress and streamline their ideas in ways in which poems do not," says songwriter and composer Rikky Rooksby. "They must simplify their language and imagery to avoid things getting too complicated to follow."[28]

Word Rhythms

Another difference between song lyrics and poems is that although both have a specific rhythm to the words, in songs the verses and the chorus are set to their own melody and rhythm. Song lyrics must therefore match the changes in

Nelly Furtado illustrates the metaphor of her song "I'm Like a Bird" during a 2007 performance.

musical notes and the overall rhythm of the song while still sounding like natural, everyday speech. "The best lyrics sound natural, like something you might say in the course of a normal conversation,"[29] says Blume. When choosing lyrics, songwriters must be as aware of the rhythm and melody of the words as they are of things like the words' meaning, imagery, and rhyme. "Your choice of a pulse or rhythmic pattern of a lyric can be just as catchy as the other elements,"[30] say songwriter Casey Kelly and music teacher David Hodge.

Stressed syllables in a song must be the same syllables that would be stressed if the lyrics were read aloud without any music at all, so words of a song cannot be forced to match the rhythm of the melody. For example, the word *cherish* has a natural stress on the first syllable, but the word *adore* has a natural stress on the second. If a word, sung to a song's melody, would naturally stress a different syllable, the word will sound unnatural. Listeners may feel that the song tries to force complicated or long words into its rhythm and melody, and the song will be difficult to understand or sing. "The stressed and unstressed syllables are mostly predetermined by the music," say Kelly and Hodge, but when words are chosen carefully for the right rhythm, they say the payoff is often a catchier tune. "Applying a strong rhythm pattern to the lyrics makes them more memorable."[31]

Pronounceable Words

Song lyrics are not meant to be read silently at the reader's leisure but to be sung aloud with the pace of the music; therefore, the singer and the listener cannot slow the rhythm down in order to pronounce complicated words.

Eminem, seen performing in 2011, is a very successful hip-hop artist who has also recorded some of the fastest raps on record. In other genres, songs with words that the listener can't understand or repeat may be very problematic.

Cramming too many words into a song or words with too many syllables makes a song hard for a singer to sing and often even harder for a listener to understand.

Rap music is one style of song in which the lyrics sometimes move too fast for the average listener to completely understand, much less repeat. In most genres, however, writing lyrics that move too fast for the song's rhythm can hurt the song's chances of ever becoming a hit. The fast words of rap music are often spoken instead of sung, but moving words along that fast to a melody in a country or R&B song would be much harder to do. Fast-moving lyrics are a problem for songs whose popularity relies on listeners' wanting to sing along to them. In such songs, listeners could get frustrated by difficult lyrics. "In most of the first songs that my clients send me, the lyrics are too bulky, and the melodies are too cluttered," says songwriter and songwriting consultant Molly-Ann Leikin. "When that happens, it's almost impossible for the melody to be memorable."[32]

This does not mean there must be just one note of the melody and one syllable of a lyric for every beat of the song. In the simple song "Yankee Doodle," there are actually seven syllables in the first four beats: the words *Yankee*, *Doodle*, and *went to* each place two syllables on a single beat, and *town* takes up a whole beat by itself. Some words can also be drawn out longer when sung to take up multiple beats of a song. Songwriters can therefore play with different words within the melody, shortening some and drawing out others. The end goal is for the song's lyrics to sound good within the notes of the melody as well as easy to sing and understand. The story of the song will be wasted if no one can make sense of the lyrics.

Lyrical Pitfalls

Songwriters must keep in mind certain pitfalls when they write the lyrics to their songs. One of these is the sounds of consonants (letters of the alphabet other than the vowels, *a*, *e*, *i*, *o*, and *u*) that are hard to say either by themselves or when paired with other consonant sounds. Words with certain sounds or sound combinations are notoriously difficult to say and could be even more difficult to sing well. The sounds of the letters *w* and *y*, as well as consonants blended with the letter *l*, for example, all have the potential to be difficult to say, creating potential tongue twisters within songs, especially if the song has a fast-paced rhythm. Also, words with too many *s* sounds, such as *hopelessness* and *circumstances*, can cause unintended whistling when the lyrics are sung; listeners may hear so much of the *s* sound that it distracts them from the actual words of the song.

Even words with the perfect meaning, rhyme, and rhythm can muddle up a lyric if they create annoying whistling sounds or tongue twisters. Adding to the difficulty of choosing just the right words for a song is the fact that repeating sounds, a practice called alliteration, can actually be a poetic device that is pleasing to the ear if used correctly. Songwriters often use alliteration as a way to make a song sound catchier. It worked in Elvis Presley's hits "Heartbreak Hotel" and "Viva Las Vegas" (1956 and 1964) and in the hard-rock band AC/DC's "Dirty Deeds Done Dirt Cheap" (1976). More recent songs that use alliteration include Carly Rae Jepsen's "Call Me Maybe" and Taylor Swift's "Begin Again," both released in 2012.

The success of such songs shows that repeated sounds can work for song titles and lyrics. However, it takes careful planning for songwriters to determine whether their use of alliteration will be catchy or troublesome for singers and listeners. "The tongue-twisting variety of lyrics may have a place in a certain kind of song," say songwriting consultants Pat and Pete Luboff, "but for the most part, for words to sing well, they must flow gently into each other."[33]

Another pitfall in lyric writing is using the wrong words for notes that are long and drawn out. If a particular word will be sung over a long note or will span several different notes, it usually sounds best if it has a long vowel such as an *o*, *e*, or *a* so the singer can carry the sound through the changes in melody. Words or syllables that have short vowel sounds and end with consonants (like *get* or *drum*) are poorly suited to long, drawn-out notes, which may be difficult or even impossible to sing well.

Carly Rae Jepsen performs at the American Music Awards in 2012. Her catchy pop hit of that year, "Call Me Maybe," uses alliteration.

"Nasal tones and consonants are almost impossible to extend," say Luboff and Luboff. "The best sounds for those long, high notes are open vowel sounds. Check out your favorite ballads and see if it isn't the case that the main sounds on the extended notes are *a, e, i, o,* and *u.*"[34] When choosing the perfect words to complete a line of lyrics, songwriters have to choose not just the words that tell the story the best, but words that can also be sung the way the melody demands.

Well-Polished Words

Settling on the perfect words to tell a song's story, create characters listeners will care about, fit perfectly with the melody, and sound good when the song is sung is a true art. When viewing song lyrics, readers are usually struck by how short the lyrics to most songs are. At first glance, it may not seem like a very time-consuming task to jot down a few rhyming lines for a song. However, a great deal of work often goes into lyric writing. The task has similarities with writing stories and writing poems, but the process of writing lyrics is unique because the words and the story also must fit within the melody and rhythm of a song. The challenge of creating well-written lyrics helps define the practice of songwriting as an art form.

CHAPTER 4

Putting the Pieces of a Song Together

The structure and notes of a melody, the blending of the right sounds for the harmony, the choice of a particular rhythm, and the selection of lyrics are all important aspects of songwriting. In some ways, each process happens on its own, apart from the others. Songwriters may come up a particular idea for a catchy rhythm or find themselves humming a few notes for a new melody. Some have an idea for a story and start with lyrics that tell about characters and situations.

New songs start out in various ways in the minds of their creators, but whatever the starting point—a string of notes, a few lines of words, or something else—it eventually must be grouped in with all the other elements of a song. Great lyrics need to be sung to melodies. Catchy melodies need lyrics to match. Both lyrics and melody must be supported by rhythm and harmony. At the end of the songwriting process, all of these elements create one complete and finished piece of art—a song.

Starting with an Idea

Thinking of songs as complete works of art helps some songwriters unify different elements like rhythm, words, and harmony. Songs are, in the end, stories. They can be

Teaming Up

Writing hit songs requires a range of skills. Successful songwriters must understand harmonies and melodies as well as rhythm and how to create good beats for songs. They need to be good storytellers, coming up with interesting situations people will relate to. They also need to have a way with words and poetic language, using clever words that paint mental pictures and are satisfying to sing.

So much goes into the process that songwriters often work in pairs or teams. One person may have a special knack at coming up with melodies and rhythms. Another might have a notebook full of song ideas and lyrics but may struggle to create great melodies. If people with different talents join to create songs, the end result is often better. Teamwork prevents a songwriter's situations, word choices,

rhythms, melodies, and harmonies from sounding the same from song to song.

Many famous songwriters have teamed up over the years: Mick Jagger and Keith Richards, Elton John and Bernie Taupin, and John Lennon and Paul McCartney are a few famous pairs. Songwriting teamwork has resulted in many award-winning and chart-topping tunes.

Bernie Taupin (left) and Elton John are among the most successful pop music songwriting duos of the twentieth century.

about real individuals but are more often about made-up characters. Nevertheless, these characters must capture the feelings or thoughts of listeners who have also had a particular experience or felt a certain way. Most songs become hits because listeners identify with their message or how the story fits into the musical elements of the song. "Putting the right lyrics into the singer's mouth creates a sense of unity and integrity that will make your listeners believe and will give real life to your song,"[35] say Pat and Pete Luboff.

To help make songs feel like believable stories, every song has a theme, a particular idea or experience or mood it is trying to create. The theme doesn't always have to be profound—there have been many silly-sounding or whimsical songs over the years—but the theme, lyrics, melody, harmony, and rhythm must work together as a whole piece of art.

To combine the different elements of a song and create what they hope will be hits, songwriters think about their future audience. People listen to music in various situations. If they are dancing or exercising, they may choose songs with a faster and more energetic rhythm. They may choose entirely different music if they are angry, sad, or trying to relax and fall asleep. Restaurants often play background music, and that music is likely to differ greatly between a fancy, black-tie bistro and a college campus burger joint. Among dance music, there are fast songs and slow ones, each designed for different kinds of movement, whether for single people to move around or for couples to sway together more slowly.

Songwriters keep in mind the purpose of the music and what most people are likely to be doing when they play a particular tune. Then they choose lyrics, rhythm, and a melody that will fit in with that purpose. "You want the feel of the music to match the feel of the lyrics," says musician Michael Miller. "If the lyrics are sad, you probably don't want to set them to a happy-sounding melody."[36]

Tunes that listeners choose for fast dancing might get away with angry lyrics, but a song that works well for slow dancing could confuse the dancers if its lyrics are not romantic. On the other hand, songs with lyrics about heartbreak may not work well with a happy, upbeat rhythm unless the point of the song is that its character is positive about moving on. "There are exceptions to this rule, of course," Miller says. "Mismatching words and lyrics can create a sense of musical irony that is appropriate in some situations—but in general, you want your melody to reflect the feel of the lyrics."[37]

Songs with lyrics that seem to fight against the mood and energy of the melody, harmony, and rhythm can certainly become hits, sometimes because they introduce an unexpected element that catches the interest of listeners. One example is Foster the People's 2011 hit "Pumped up Kicks," whose upbeat, whimsical melody sent it to number one on the *Billboard* charts even though the lyrics speak to a teenager plotting to shoot at his peers. Despite the rare popularity of such hits, songwriters typically stick to a certain theme or mood for their song in its melody, rhythm, and lyrics.

The Shape of a Song

When all the pieces of a song work well together under a common theme, the song works like a short trip through time. Like any story, most songs start with a character who faces some problem or challenge, struggles with it, and emerges at the end having solved the problem or learned to see the things differently because of it. In addition to having a theme, most songs follow a dome-shaped story arc similar to almost any story, novel, or movie—the action starts low as the story, characters, and problem are introduced, and then the energy, excitement, and suspense build as the character gets closer to the climax of the story. Then the action and momentum of the story drop off again to a calmer level once the character has faced the problem, so that the story ends at a level of calmness much like where it started.

The lyrics of a song often tell most of the story, but the melody, harmony, and rhythm echo the character's journey and the story arc. They usually start out at a certain pace and

The American Pop Song Form

One of the most common song forms in American pop music is known as AABA. The song structure is also called ballad form or thirty-two bar form. Within this format, there are four sections, and each section of the song has eight bars. The A section is referred to as the verse, and the B section is referred to as the bridge. The musician's resource website Songstuff explains why the AABA format is so popular:

The first eight bars (A) is a statement of melodic theme so catchy, so cool and lovely, that we want to hear it again. And so the second eight bars (A) repeats it. Then, before such repetition has a chance to become cloying or boring, the third eight bars introduces harmonic variation and another melody (B), which leads right back to a welcome return of the original melodic phrase (A) as the final eight bars of the chorus. . . .

This pattern is so pleasing and effective that it became a standard model favored not only by those great old dead guys like [George and Ira] Gershwin, Cole Porter, [Richard] Rodgers and [Lorenz] Hart, et al, but also by [the Beatles' John] Lennon and [Paul] McCartney.

Songstuff. "A Rough Guide to the History of Songwriting Language." http://song writing.songstuff.com/article/songwriting_terminology.

with a certain tone. The tempo might increase as the story gets closer to its climax, and the melody and harmony almost always rise as the song progresses, reaching their highest and loudest point—a crescendo—during the moment of the song where the character is facing the biggest crisis or learning the biggest lesson. John Stevens, a songwriting professor who has developed college courses to help students explore the music of John Lennon and the Beatles, explains:

> Songs tell a story or communicate a point. Each part of the song has a particular role in telling the story. Most songs have a beginning to set the stage, a middle in which the story is developed further, and an end, or conclusion. Somewhere in between, the music and the lyrics build to reach a climax or high point, and that is where we discover the point, punch line, or moral to the story.[38]

Having songs occur in a story arc leads to a typical song structure on which countless songwriters rely. Songs often begin with a verse that includes the introduction to the character and problem of the song story. They then move into a chorus, which captures the meaning or message of the song. The chorus is followed by another verse in which the character is moving up the hill of the story arc. This second verse may be followed by another chorus, which is usually a repetition of the first one, showing that the character struggled but still has the same problem or misunderstanding.

By now, the song is usually nearing the top of the story arc. The character must resolve the problem or come to terms with it somehow. There may be what is called a bridge—a part of a song with notes, harmony, rhythm, and lyrics that differ from either the verses or the chorus. The bridge, if a song has one, shows the character changing somehow. It is usually followed by another chorus, often sung louder and at a higher pitch than the previous choruses. This is the climax of the song—its most exciting and thrilling part.

After this energetic or high-pitched chorus, the song's tempo and melody usually scale back down toward where they were at the beginning of the song. In the lyrics, the chorus may be repeated more quietly to drive home the point of

what the character learned (or sometimes, that the character was defeated by the problem), or there may be a new verse that shows how the character is different than at the beginning of the song, such as being wiser, more determined to succeed, or just more accepting of the way things have to be.

Character Growth and Change

People who listen to songs expect this story arc to happen, much the way they expect a story, novel, or movie to follow a certain pattern of starting slow, building to a peak, and then resolving by the end. A catchy rhythm, melody, or string of lyrics may be a good beginning to a song, but songwriters have to put all the pieces together to build a story in every song, one that rises to a high moment of action and then drops back down to where it started. Each verse must say something new and show the character growing or changing. Most successful songs are not merely a series of repetitive verses and choruses that all say the same thing because these would not show the character growing or changing.

Something new needs to happen in each verse of a song, such as starting out by telling how the couple met and then moving on to tell how they started dating. By the climax, something exciting should happen (they decide to get married) or something unexpected should take place (they break up, or a tragedy happens that keeps them apart). By the last verse of the song, the character has gone through some change and accepted either a different life or the same life as before. A good song, like any good story, is more than a laundry list of different reasons why the character feels or is a certain way. It shows how things have changed for the character over a period of time.

Understanding the Expectations

Just as song lyrics need to happen in some kind of progression, a song's melodies and harmonies cannot simply be a repeat of the same thing over and over. Listeners pay attention to the way a song's sound moves forward, even if they do not realize it. As the melody and harmony rise, it helps the listener understand that the song is getting closer to the point it is trying to make. When the song reaches a crescendo, usually with the loudest and highest notes, the listener understands that the song is nearing its end. As the energy of the song rises, so does the listener's attention to it. After the climax, as the song slows down and goes back to the lower notes and the slower rhythm with which it started, the listener feels like the journey is now complete.

Without dramatic changes in the song's rhythm or rises in the song's volume and the notes of its melody and harmony, listeners may grow frustrated with a song. It will seem to travel along in a straight line with no indication that it is nearing its end. Songs without an arc risk being boring, repetitive, and even annoying, to listeners who expect a song to rise in action and energy, get to its point, and then come to an end.

Most people listen to their favorite songs over and over again. If a song has no changes in pitch, volume, melody, and rhythm to indicate a climax, most listeners probably will not find it appealing enough repeat. "When you set the stage in a song, you will create expectations for the listener

Claiming Singer-Songwriter Status

Songwriting has long been considered a separate art from performing. Songwriters are not always talented at performing their creations, and performing artists often choose songs from songwriters they can perform in their own style. Increasingly, however, singers choose to write their own melodies and lyrics. They know the musical styles they like, the kinds of stories they want to tell as artists, and their performing talents and weaknesses.

Singer-songwriters have created innovative, popular, and memorable music over the years, but the practice of writing and performing one's own songs is not without controversy. When singers claim songwriting credits for their hits, they are entitled to songwriting profits. Some songwriters, however, claim that some performers change as little as one or two words in a lyric or a few notes of a melody and claim credit as co-writers of the entire song. Hit songs can generate a lot of money for songwriters, a possible incentive for songwriters and performing artists alike to claim a bigger role in the songwriting process. But performing artists may also be considered more talented if they write their own material instead of singing someone else's, so singer-songwriter status is coveted in the industry.

that something in particular is going to happen," says songwriter Ralph Murphy. "Obviously, you can use those expectations to good effect to surprise the listener with a twist in the narrative of the song, but somehow, someway you will need to provide the listener with some sort of resolution."[39]

Hard work and a clear understanding of music ensure that a song's musical story arc works as well as the lyrics to give listening audiences the kind of story progression they expect. Audiences are fickle, so there are examples of songs that have become hits despite breaking these "rules" of songwriting. But songwriters, especially when they are just starting out, need to understand that songs are stories, and how melodies, harmonies, rhythm, and lyrics work together to build a song to a crescendo.

Writing Standout Songs

Following the general expectations for good music is important to songwriting, but there is no one formula for all songwriters to follow. As they gain experience, most songwriters like to experiment with sounds and ideas that will make their work different from the millions of songs that have come before. Because there are only a limited number of themes and musical notes available, coming up with a completely original song can be a challenge. "It's almost impossible to be totally original when it comes to a song topic," say Casey Kelly and David Hodge. "After all, over the past two thousand years or so, songs have been written about almost every subject you can think of."[40]

Song melodies and harmonies also run the risk of sounding similar to other tunes. However, Kelly and Hodge say each songwriter's originality and creativity make a difference. "The cool thing about songwriting is that even when you're writing about something other people have written about, it's *you* doing the writing. And the world has yet to hear from you."[41]

To avoid mimicking other songs, which often happens by accident, songwriters often tweak the other elements of a song's sound. Listeners, often without realizing it, have certain expectations when they hear music. Certain harmonies go so well together, for example, that people become used to hearing them in order. A song's melody often repeats itself too, during the verses and the chorus, and listeners expect most songs to follow the arc pattern, building in tempo and pitch toward the climax. Rhythm, likewise, can become predictable in song. The same drum beat often carries through an entire song from start to finish, like a pulse.

Songwriters can suddenly throw a kink into any of these expected elements, such as altering the rhythm at a key point in the song. These changes can be risky if they jar the listener too much and make a song unsatisfying. Done well, though, such unexpected elements, or syncopation, can be exciting, because they take a song in a unique direction the listener was not expecting. "Let syncopation into your music," advises singer-songwriter Michael Lydon. "The fun makes the risk worthwhile, and there's nothing like syncopated [song elements] to lift listeners' spirits and get them up out of their seats and dancing."[42]

Another way for songwriters to make songs distinct is to imagine them being played in a particular style or with a particular instrument. Someone writing a rap song, for example, may include a part of the song that will be sung and a part that will be rapped, or spoken portions may be added to songs that are mostly intended to be sung. A songwriter may also indicate that particular kinds of instruments should be used, such as a fiddle, a harmonica, or a particular type of drum to give songs a unique sound that goes along with the theme. Songwriters sometimes indicate such things when writing their music to help their songs stand out.

Sometimes, of course, the songwriter has little to do with the actual final sound of a song. The melody, harmony, and lyrics are often presented to a particular band or singer, and these artists shape the song in different ways to make it unique and distinctly their own. The same song will probably sound very different depending on whether it is performed by a rock band, a country singer, or a hip-hop artist, and sometimes the same song can be recorded by all three.

During the actual performing and recording of a song, it often changes a great deal. Performing artists give songs

The performance and recording of a song can change it significantly from the songwriter's original intention.

their own unique twist, which can help certain tunes stand out from similar-sounding ones. The songwriter is responsible for making his or her music interesting and different, adding unique elements such as syncopation to make songs appeal to the people who might sing them. However, original songs usually must be strong enough to catch people's interest even when played and sung without sound effects or the musical talents of a world-class singer or band. Good songs simply have to sound good, however they are sung.

Grabbing the Listener's Attention

Songwriters may spend many hours imagining how their song will sound on the radio someday, but the hard work that goes into creating a song will be wasted if it does not have something that gets a listener's attention. This is what professionals in the music industry call a *hook*. A song has to grab listeners, keep them interested for the entire song, and leave them remembering (possibly even singing) the song. A song without a great hook, preferably one that comes up soon after it begins, may be doomed. Listeners rarely if ever wait until the very end of a song to decide if they like it. If nothing happens early in the song to get their attention, they are quick to change the radio station or skip to the next tune on a playlist.

Industry professionals know this, too. When a new song comes to producers, they search for some kind of hook that grabs their attention and will appeal to millions of other listeners. Without a good hook that happens early on, a song may never be heard in its entirety. "You won't be given long to hit the listener with what is presumably your best shot,"[43] says songwriter and producer Eric Beall.

Unfortunately for songwriters, a hook is hard to define, and there is no formula for creating a great one. Syncopation sometimes goes hand in hand with creating a great hook, because a song with something unexpected and catchy will likely make listeners perk up and want to hear more. A hook is generally a particular rhythm, piece of melody, or string of lyrics that becomes a repeated element of the song. Many different things can work as the song's hook, but it has to happen fairly early on—an exciting element that does not happen until the end of the song will never be heard by listeners who have already turned it off. Songs with good hooks are recognizable, because hooks are memorable. The point of the hook is to catch an audience's attention and make them want to hear the song again. "The essence of a good song is that the listener walks away singing the hook,"[44] says Pamela Phillips Oland.

Whether a hook is a bit of melody, a catchy rhythm, a memorable line of lyrics, or a combination of things, it is usually short, appealing, and easy to remember. Hooks that are part of a melody may span no more than a dozen notes. Hooks that are lyrics can vary in length from one word (perhaps repeated often in the song or drawn out over various notes when sung aloud) to a string of words. The more words that are strung together in a hook, the more fun they usually have to be to sing in order to grab an audience's attention. Short strings of lyrics tend to work better as hooks.

A hook that is mostly linked to rhythm may be the most difficult to pull off because it cannot be hummed or sung out loud. Nevertheless, some songs do have successful rhythmic hooks, especially if a recognizable rhythm can be tapped or clapped out. For example, the 1994 hit "I'll Be There for You" by the Rembrandts was the theme song for the popular 1990s–2000s TV series *Friends*, and its hook was a fast, four-beat clap after the first line of lyrics. Queen's 1977 hit "We Will Rock You" is still an anthem at sporting events for its widely known rhythmic hook of two stomps and a clap.

Whatever element is used as the hook, almost every professional in the music industry agrees that a successful song absolutely must have one. "I can't adequately express how important the 'hook' of a song actually is," says songwriting consultant Rick Dean. "A good hook can and does make or break a song, it's that simple. It can be the difference of suc-

An elaborate performance of "We Will Rock You" was staged at a 2005 soccer match in Munich, Germany. The song's simple and unique hook has contributed to its ongoing worldwide success since 1977.

cess or failure."[45] Whether successful songwriters begin their creative process with lyrics, melody, or rhythm, the piece they start with is usually a potential hook, and they build the song around this catchy component so that listeners can sing, hum, or clap part of the song every time they hear it.

Naming the Finished Product

A hook is like a song's memory flag, and virtually all successful songs have one. Before a song is ever marketed to potential publishers or to the public, however, it needs one final touch—a great title. Sometimes, naming a song is the last thing a songwriter does, and sometimes, it is one of the first. This is because a song's title is often very closely related to its hook, or at least to the chorus. A song's title is almost always a word or a phrase that is repeated often in the song. If a song's hook is found in its lyrics, that hook makes a good basis of the song's title as well. For example, in Katy Perry's 2012 number-one hit "Wide Awake," the song title is also the hook and includes the first words listeners hear in the song.

If the hook is a rhythm or a melody instead of lyrics, the song title is usually taken from part of the chorus. That way the title is repeated often enough to be memorable and to capture the theme of the song. Choosing a song's title wisely is very important to its overall future success. Songs with great lyrics, catchy melodies and rhythms, and a perfect hook are often poised to become popular hits, and when listeners hear a song for the first time on the radio, they may want to hear it again. In order to find the song and buy it, they need to know its title, and that is easiest to guess when the title is either the hook or an obvious part of the lyrics repeated through the song. "Sometimes titles are repeated over and over," say music industry professionals Jim Peterik, Dave Austin, and Cathy Lynn. "This placement and repetition drives the title home to the listeners so they can ask their friends, 'Did you hear such-and-such on the radio?'"[46]

Some hits have become successful even when their titles do not match the lyrics or when the words of the title are

Foster the People performs in San Francisco, California, in 2011. The words "Helena Beat" are never said in singer Mark Foster's (center) hit song of the same name.

never said within the song. Some examples are "Helena Beat" by Foster the People (2011) and Queen's rock anthem "Bohemian Rhapsody," which was released in 1975 but is still popular enough to have amassed 3 million digital downloads by October 2012. In 1993 rock band Pearl Jam released "Elderly Woman Behind the Counter in a Small Town," which was a top-twenty hit on the rock charts despite a cumbersome title that was never mentioned in the song. There are many other examples of hits that have peculiar titles, but in general, most listeners appreciate song titles that make the tune easy to find online and download digitally as long as they know a portion of the lyrics.

For songwriters and artists, song titles are important because song sales determine a song's popularity and financial success. Customers must be able to identify a song in order to buy it. "In most cases, it's what you make of a title that separates an average song from a great one,"[47] say Peterik, Austin, and Lynn. When all the pieces of a song work perfectly together, including its title, a songwriter's hope is that the music will be recorded, released, and his or her work of art will be heard by the world.

CHAPTER 5

The Business of Songwriting

Not all songwriters are professional musicians, and many people create songs for reasons that have nothing to do with getting published or hearing their work on the radio. However, most songwriters create music because they want the world to hear and hum along with their creations. They hope to write popular tunes that will become hits and be heard for years or decades.

Some songwriters work part time at their craft and find full-time employment elsewhere (perhaps not even in the music industry). Others aim to become career songwriters who make a living by creating and selling music. Reaching a professional level of songwriting, where one gets paid for his or her artistic creations, is both possible and rewarding, but achieving that level of success is not easy. It takes talent, hard work, perseverance, and knowledge of how the music industry works. Most professional songwriters spend their entire careers learning about this constantly changing industry so that their musical creations and their business approach stay relevant.

Learning the Craft of Songwriting

Songwriters, like musicians and singers, come from all different backgrounds. As the world has seen from talent

Formal instruction in music and music theory is helpful, but not crucial, for developing songwriting skills. Many songwriters are self-taught musicians.

discovery shows like *American Idol*, *The Voice*, and *The X Factor*, talented musicians are found everywhere. Kelly Clarkson, winner of *American Idol*'s first season, was living out of her car when she auditioned for the show because her Los Angeles apartment building had just burned down. Chris Daughtry, whose career as a rock musician was launched after he was the fourth-place contestant on *American Idol*'s fifth season, worked at a car dealership at the time of his *Idol* audition. Both singers now have successful music careers and co-write many of their own hits.

The success of artists on TV programs like *American Idol* proves that there are many different paths to a music career. Unlike many professions, such as becoming a doctor or lawyer, careers in music do not necessarily begin with a particular college degree, license, or certification. Anybody from anywhere has the potential to create hit songs. "Somehow many of us are taught that we can't write songs, that it takes some sort of individual who has special training," says songwriter and music business professor Dick Weissman. "I honestly believe that anyone can write a song."[48]

This is not to say that songwriters do not need to know anything about music. Most songwriters seem to have an instinctive understanding of music and have learned to sing, play instruments, or both. Songwriters can usually recreate certain strings of melodies or harmonies simply by hearing them, and they know what notes go well together to make even more interesting melodies and harmonies. People interested in music often learn by doing—they experiment with putting sounds together. They may also take music lessons to learn how to put together rhythms and harmonies. Most of all, songwriting hopefuls listen to many different kinds of music to learn what they like and dislike, how popular songs are structured, and why certain songs become big hits.

Songwriters may also benefit from learning about creative writing and poetry. Crafting meaningful lyrics is a big part of songwriting, and good poets share many characteristics with good songwriters—they tell stories in few words, they construct creative and memorable images, and they use techniques like rhythm and rhyme to give a smooth and logical sound to their message. Songwriters who develop the skills and habits of good storytellers and poets have more tools to use when trying to craft the perfect lyrics for their songs.

Taking courses or even getting a college degree in a subject like musical theory or creative writing can help songwriters improve their craft, but many successful songwriters are entirely self-taught. They read books and talk to experienced writers and musicians. They combine their love and appreciation for music with the skills and knowledge they gather. Most of all, they practice. They put all of this knowledge to use in the creation of new and even better songs.

Sharing Songs

Fitting all the pieces of a song together usually takes a lot of time and effort on the part of the songwriter. Songs may only last a few minutes, but the process of creating them can take weeks, months, and in some cases, years. "The reality is that most songs need to be coaxed into being," say

Copyrights for Songwriters

Songwriters often collaborate with one another, play their original music at public events, post songs on the Internet, and pass out copies of their work to industry professionals. To protect their songs from being stolen by other people, songwriters often copyright their work.

A copyright is a declaration that a creative work is the property of the person who created it. By U.S. law, copyrights are automatic—the moment someone puts a creative idea into a physical form, such as writing it down or recording it, it is copyrighted to its creator. Songwriters can make this legally official by registering their songs with the U.S. Copyright Office in Washington, D.C. Once they have a registered copyright, they have a strong legal basis to challenge anyone who tries to claim the exact same song.

Copyrights are important in the songwriting industry. Writers may sell their copyright to a music publisher, for example, meaning that the publisher now owns the song. (It is similar to selling a car or another tangible thing.) Giving up a copyright is usually an advantage for a songwriter, however, because in exchange, he or she will get paid.

Casey Kelly and David Hodge.[49] A song usually starts out as an idea—from an interesting melody or a line or two of lyrics—but building the rest of the song around this starting point can be a long process. Most songwriters also spend a lot of time revising their songs, working to find just the right word or phrase of lyrics to convey what they want to say or tweaking bits of the melody or harmony to make them shift more smoothly.

By the end of the process, songwriters usually go through several versions of every song they create. Most songwriters also work on more than one song at a time. In order to keep the numerous versions of their songs straight, songwriters usually record their songs, so they remember how each one is supposed to sound. The final version of a song is usually recorded as a *demonstration*, or demo. This is what the songwriter will use to share the new tune with people who might be interested in buying or performing it. Ultimately, songwriters who have learned the ins and outs of their craft must also learn how to get their songs heard by the people who will buy them.

"Almost anyone can write a song," says career expert Shelly Field. "Selling it or publishing it is a different matter."[50] A good songwriter could come from virtually any background, and most industry professionals care less about who the particular songwriter is than about the quality of the songs he or she is able to produce. Breaking into a songwriting career requires not just brilliant art but also a great deal of business savvy.

Demonstrating Song Skills

Demos are an important step in presenting one's musical creations to potential buyers. They are usually recorded as digital sound files. These can be stored in the songwriter's computer and shared in a variety of ways. Sound files can be emailed, and they can also be posted to a website. Those who want to hear the song can easily download the file. The Internet is a useful way for songwriters to share their creations. They can get a lot more exposure from emailing their songs or posting music on websites than planning to meet music industry professionals in person and hand them a physical copy of the song. Of course, digital music files can still be burned onto compact discs (CDs) and handed out, too. Songwriters experiment with many different ways to get their musical creations out to the world, because unless the right person hears and loves the song, no one is going to buy it.

Making a great demo is one of the most important things a songwriter can do if he or she hopes to make a career out of songwriting. The music industry is extremely competitive, and the people who buy and publish songs listen to countless tunes in the search for the handful that they actually end up buying from songwriters. "Suffice it to say, whether you're an accomplished professional, an amateur with grand ambitions, or a musical weekend warrior, you're not alone," says Eric Beall. "There's close to half a million people out there who share the dream."[51] In the face of such stiff competition, every demo must be the best it can be. Sometimes, a songwriter has enough talent as a singer and a musician to perform the song in the demo himself. Often, though, songwriters realize their own talents as musicians might not impress the people who will listen to their demo. They may enlist the help of musicians they know to play instruments and sing the song for their demo.

Having good musicians and singers who make a new song sound its best is important in creating a demo and so is quality recording equipment. Most modern computers have built-in microphones and can record sound files to the

Going Digital

The world has seen a digital revolution in recent years. Products once available only as hard copies—such as books, magazines, movies, and albums—are now processed as digital information files that can be downloaded by any computer. The ability to download digital versions of songs has had major effects on the music industry, changing the nature of how people consume and listen to music and how artists get paid for it. Recording artists have traditionally made albums containing groups of songs, usually only a few of which are released as singles to be played on the radio. Fans once had to buy an entire album in order to have a copy of a favorite song. This gave singers and bands the ability to experiment with songs that would not necessarily become hits. As long as they had at least one big hit on an album, all of the album's cuts would sell well. Nowadays, with digital music, people tend to buy fewer albums and more of the singles they like. This puts pressure on songwriters and recording artists to create all smash hits, because experimental songs may not sell in the digital market or earn anyone much money.

A microphone, amplifier, guitar, computer, and recording software are all that many songwriters use to record demos and sell their songs.

computer, but the end recording may be of very poor quality when it is converted to a sound file. Songs may sound tinny or fuzzy if recorded this way, and even good songs performed by talented musicians will not sound very professional in the demo file.

Serious songwriters often invest in quality recording equipment for their music so that their demos have a clear, rich sound. Some songwriters even use professional recording studios to make their demos. Many people believe that a brilliant song will eventually find its way to large audiences, but faced with tremendous competition, songwriters often take steps to ensure their demos reflect what they imagine the song should sound like when sung by professional recording artists. "They [demos] are meant to give music industry professionals a way to hear all the elements of your song as clearly as possible so they can decide if it has commercial potential,"[52] say the editors of *Songwriter's Market*.

Selling a Song

After a song has been written and a demo of it has been distributed, songwriters wait to hear back from someone who wants to buy their song. Usually, this will be a music publisher—a company that buys songs from songwriters and then distributes those songs to paying markets. A music publisher may have thousands of songs in its catalog. Companies that need new musical material often seek out music publishers and see what they have to offer. These companies can range from advertising agencies to television shows to representatives of recording artists who are looking for songs to put on a new album. Music publishers acquire new songs all the time to add to their catalogs, and songwriters must publish their songs in order to sell tunes to recording artists. "Under copyright law, every song has to be published," says music publisher Sherry Bond. "Even if you write a song and your best friend Garth Brooks records it, you still have to have a publisher for your song."[53]

Music publishers range in size and reputation in the industry. Some, like Universal, Sony, and Warner, are larger and better known, and these may be the publishers big-name recording artists go to when looking for new songs to sing. Other publishers are smaller, and they may mostly serve newer recording artists who have not yet had major hits. Even though song publishers keep thousands of songs on file and are always looking for exciting new songs, it can be very difficult for a breakout songwriter to sell a new song to a publisher. This is because most large publishers also have staff writers, experienced songwriters who can quickly generate the kinds of songs a particular recording artist might be seeking, such as a country ballad about being homesick or a rock anthem about breaking free of stereotypes.

Furthermore, although music publishers try to pitch their best songs to recording artists, they, too, face stiff competition from other publishers. A song might seem just right for a particular artist's next album, but it might be one of a hundred songs the artist is considering. Most new albums contain only about ten or twelve songs, and some of those are often songs the artist either wrote or co-wrote for his or her own album. Only some of the songs from the thousands of tunes publishers own make it onto new albums at all. The bigger the star who will be recording the song, the stiffer the competition, and the harder it is for a songwriter's creation to land in one of the album's few available spots.

As difficult as it is to sell a song to a publisher, songwriters can have success if their songs are very well written and original enough that the publisher believes they could become hits. If a songwriter's music lands in a publisher's catalog, it brings the songwriter one step closer to the possibility of having his or her first great hit, because it is possible that a recording artist will choose that song and make it popular for millions of listeners.

Royalties and Song Ownership

A publisher buys songs from independent songwriters, or in some cases, pays its staff of songwriters to create a new song. Once a publisher pays a songwriter for music, the song becomes the property of the publisher, who in turn tries to sell the song to a recording artist, who buys it for a fee. (The recording artists do not usually handle the task

The iTunes Store is projected behind Steve Jobs, the chief executive officer of Apple, at a 2004 presentation. The service sells songs as digital downloads, and a portion of each sale goes to the songwriter.

by themselves. They answer to record labels, the executives of which have their own opinions about what songs will end up on albums and handle much of the business side of purchasing songs from publishers.) Once a recording artist makes an album or a single out of the song and that song is released to the public, all the various people who have had something to do with creating the song take a share of its profits.

Every time a song is purchased as a single on the Internet or by radio stations that intend to play the song, money is exchanged. The recording artist or band gets paid and so do the artist's record label and representatives. The publisher of the song takes a share of the profits, too, and pays half of this share to the songwriter. Who gets paid and who gets the credit for writing the song are determined by legal contracts between the various people and companies involved in the process. In the end, a songwriter whose song is chosen and recorded by a performer gets a share of the money the song earns whenever it is played on the radio or sold as a single or part of an album. This share of money is called a royalty, and it is the main way songwriters get paid.

If a song becomes a big hit and sells millions of copies, the songwriter gets a portion of money every time the song is played or performed—no matter who is singing or performing it. This means songwriters must also be prepared to be businesspeople long term. "The reality is that this is the music *business*," says Jason Blume. "If your goal is to be successful in the music business, you have to pay as much attention to the *business* as you do to the *music*."[54]

Economic Reality for Songwriters

Writing a song that becomes a big hit for a recording artist is a difficult feat. The song has to be chosen by a publisher and then by the performer and all the people the performer works with. Even if a song overcomes huge odds and makes it this far, it ultimately faces one final test of judgment by the public. Fans must listen to the song, like it, and choose to buy it. Songwriters do stand to make a great deal of money if recording artists turn their songs into major successes. "A massive hit like [Adele's] 'Rolling in the Deep' or [Lady Gaga's] 'Poker Face' can make [a songwriter] as much as $500,000 per year just in radio royalties,"[55] says Steve Knopper of *Rolling Stone* magazine. He says Rihanna's 2007 hit "Umbrella" earned more than $600,000 for its songwriters by the time it sold 4 million copies (although that sum had to be split four ways because the song had four co-writers).

Despite such success stories, most songwriters do not become wealthy, especially off a single song. Songs that sell a million copies clearly do not earn a songwriter a million dollars. The songwriter only gets a small share of the song's total earnings, because the proceeds are split between so many different people. It may take months for the makers of a song, even a reasonably big hit, to earn revenue. Royalties are paid out in segments, typically either quarterly (four times a year) or semiannually (twice a year). Songwriters with lesser-performing songs may reasonably expect to earn only a few thousand dollars in royalties per song.

A single, even if it is reasonably successful, will not necessarily make the songwriter rich. But if songwriters have multiple successful songs, all earning royalties at the same time, they stand to earn a very good living at their craft. "Our government mandates songwriters get paid 9.1 cents per unit sold," says finance expert Kenneth Fisher. "So write one song on an album selling a million copies, you get $91,000. If you write all the songs—maybe 12—that can be over $1 million."[56] Songwriters serious about making a career out of their skills aim to write and sell many songs in the course of their lifetime.

Avoiding the One-Hit Wonder

Breaking into the music business and having a big hit is a difficult accomplishment, but a songwriter who has success with one song usually finds it easier to sell future songs. The songwriter has name recognition and a song credit, making him or her familiar to professionals in the industry. They may be interested in hearing other things he or she has written. Writing one hit song, however, does not guarantee success with future songs. Even songwriters who have written numerous hits often find that their songs frequently get passed on. "Many songs that ended up being major hits were turned down a dozen or more times by famous artists and producers," Weissman says.[57]

Songwriters who do make a living at their craft must continue working hard and being creative, coming up with new songs all the time. The more songs they write to sell, the greater the odds that one of those songs will surpass the stiff competition to become a hit single. Some songwriters are able to land a staff writing position for a publisher, where they write songs at the request of recording artists and other industry professionals. Although staff writing jobs are hard to find, they do guarantee a reliable source of income. Whether working on a publisher's staff or not, successful songwriters must be prolific, meaning they write many songs, often for different genres or markets. They are usually willing and able to write for anyone who wants to pay them for their songs. Making money on numerous songs generates a more reliable income than hoping to make a lot of money on just one song.

For this reason, songwriters try hard to avoid being one-hit wonders, a term that refers to people who create one popular song and never have another big hit. Getting any song recorded by any artist is a big accomplishment in such a competitive field, but most aspiring songwriters want many hit songs during their career. What the public buys determines whether a song will be popular, but most songwriters also aim for even higher standards of approval, especially from their peers in the music business. Most career songwriters strive for both popular *and* award-winning, creative songs.

What Makes an Award-Winning Song?

Most of the fame and fortune in the music business goes to the artists who perform songs. However catchy or meaningful a melody, however moving its lyrics, it is ultimately the recording artist who performs the song and makes it a

The Songwriters Hall of Fame

Induction into the Songwriters Hall of Fame (SHoF) is one of the most prestigious honors songwriters can achieve. The SHoF was established in 1969 to honor artists whose songwriting work has resulted in a wide spectrum of popular music hits. As of 2010, fewer than four hundred songwriters had earned a place in the SHoF.

Every June, the week before the induction ceremony for the year's hall-of-fame honorees is declared Songwriters Hall of Fame Week. Classes, seminars, and workshops for songwriters of all skill levels are held throughout the event. Since 2010, the SHoF has also had a physical location in the Los Angeles Grammy Museum. Visitors can learn about the work of every hall-of-fame member and try their hand at songwriting with interactive kiosks. The SHoF is widely respected as a major supporter of the work of songwriters everywhere.

Kanye West (left) inducts John Legend into the Songwriters Hall of Fame in 2007.

hit. Some songs even become hits many times over because they are performed by different artists. It might become a country song, a rock tune, or a dance hit, because artists take the basic elements of a song (lyrics, melody, harmony, rhythm) and add their own touches, often recording it very differently than anyone else. The original songwriter still gets credit for coming up with the song, so a tune that appeals to listeners in different genres has a greater chance of becoming a big hit.

Writing a song that can become a hit in more than one genre is one way for a songwriter to become known in the industry. It demonstrates that he or she can write songs that multiple artists in different genres can identify with and songs that will appeal to wide audiences. Performing artists often take liberties with songs, sometimes slightly changing lyrics (such as making a first-person song into a second-person song or changing it from a song for a female narrator to one from a male's point of view). Performers may also change some of the original melody, harmony, or rhythm to make a song uniquely their own. Just the same, the songwriter who created the original piece of music will gain respect in the industry for laying the groundwork for many successful interpretations.

Writing a song that becomes a hit, especially on multiple charts, is one way a songwriter's career can advance, because they get to take credit for writing the song, no matter where it appears or who performs it. Another way for songwriters to achieve recognition in the music industry is when one of their recorded songs wins a major award, such as a Grammy. Since 1958, an organization of music professionals and experts called the National Academy of Recording Arts and Sciences has selected songs annually for Grammy awards. The songs, albums, and performances that win Grammys are chosen based on a variety of factors, but winners are not necessarily the most popular songs during a given year. Members of the academy look at many factors in choosing Grammy winners, and although they look mostly at the artist's final performance of the song, an artistically written song has a chance to be nominated even if it is not a favorite among the listening audiences.

Grammy awards show a level of appreciation for great music by successful professionals in the industry. A songwriter whose work wins this special recognition usually earns a special level of respect. Recording artists, often seeking not just big hits but big awards for their music, may consider recording other tunes from a Grammy-winning songwriter. Out of thousands of songs recorded and sung every year, awards like Grammys go to only a few. Winning such an award is not easy, but it is one of the major ways for songwriters to set themselves apart and make themselves bigger contenders in the highly competitive music industry.

Singer-songwriter Adele holds the six awards she won at the 2012 Grammys. Winning a Grammy grants songwriters a higher level of acclaim and recognition in the industry.

The Future of Songwriting

People who dream of writing songs face many challenges. Coming up with creative, original music is only a part of the process. Songwriters who wish to hear their music on the radio must not only have talent, creativity, and an understanding of what makes songs successful but also a great deal of patience and perseverance. Just breaking into the music industry can be difficult and going on to write additional successful songs takes a great deal of dedication.

Those whose songs do become hits, however, have a very important role in society. Music is one of the ways people make sense of their lives, share experiences, understand each other, and get through difficult times. Songwriters have a special gift when they can capture feelings and trends and put them into song. They are, in a way, the spokespeople of their generation, because the songs people listen to become a central part of modern culture. Songwriting is a difficult process, but those who undertake it are in a position to create songs that will define the current generation for many years to come.

NOTES

Chapter 1: The History of American Pop Music

1. Marcel Danesi. *Popular Culture: Introductory Perspectives*, second edition. Plymouth, UK: Rowman & Littlefield, 2012, p. 13.
2. Danesi. *Popular Culture: Introductory Perspectives*, p. 117.
3. Kate Van Winkle Keller with John Koegel. "Secular Music to 1800." In *The Cambridge History of American Music*, edited by David Nicholls. New York: Cambridge University Press, 1998, p. 49.
4. Timothy D. Taylor. "Music Technologies in Everyday Life." In *Music, Sound, and Technology in America: A Documentary History of Early Phonograph, Cinema, and Radio*, edited by Timothy D. Taylor, Mark Katz, and Tony Grajeda. Durham, NC: Duke University Press, 2012, pp. 3, 5.
5. Cleve Francis. "Country and Black Listeners: Not an Oxymoron." *Billboard*, February 4, 1995, p. 5.
6. Michael Campbell and James Brody. *Rock and Roll: An Introduction*. Belmont, CA: Thomson Schirmer, 2008, p. 10.
7. Campbell and Brody. *Rock and Roll: An Introduction*, p. 10.
8. Philip V. Bohlman. "Immigrant, Folk, and Regional Musics in the Twentieth Century." In *The Cambridge History of American Music*, edited by David Nicholls. New York: Cambridge University Press, 1998, pp. 285–286.
9. David Dicaire. *Jazz Musicians of the Early Years, to 1945*. Jefferson, NC: McFarland & Company, 2002, p. 13.
10. Matthew C. Whitaker, ed. *Icons of Black America, Volume 2: Breaking Barriers and Crossing Boundaries*. Santa Barbara, CA: Greenwood, 2011, p. 616.
11. Albin J. Zak III. "Foreword." In Frank W. Hoffmann. *Rhythm and Blues, Rap, and Hip-Hop*. New York: Facts On File, 2006, p. viii.

Chapter 2: Melody, Harmony, and Rhythm

12. Jack Perricone. *Melody in Songwriting: Tools and Techniques for Writing Hit Songs*. Boston: Berklee, 2000, p. 2.
13. Perricone. *Melody in Songwriting: Tools and Techniques for Writing Hit Songs*, p. vii.

14. Craig M. Wright. *Listening to Music*, sixth edition. Boston: Schirmer, 2011, pp. 37–38.
15. Wright. *Listening to Music*, p. 39.
16. William Duckworth. *A Creative Approach to Music Fundamentals*, eleventh edition. Boston: Schirmer, 2011, p. 4.
17. Duckworth. *A Creative Approach to Music Fundamentals*, p. 7.
18. Campbell and Brody. *Rock and Roll: An Introduction*, p. 9.
19. Campbell and Brody, *Rock and Roll: An Introduction*, p. 9.
20. Quoted in Simon Frith. *Performing Rites: On the Value of Popular Music*. Cambridge, MA: Boston University Press, 1996, p. 270.
21. Quoted in Frith. *Performing Rites: On the Value of Popular Music*, p. 270.
22. Elizabeth C. Axford. *Song Sheets to Software: A Guide to Print Music, Software, and Websites for Musicians*, second edition. Oxford, UK: Scarecrow, 2004, p. 38.

Chapter 3: All in the Words

23. Gary Burns. "Trends in Lyrics in the Annual Top Twenty Songs in the United States, 1963–1972." In *American Popular Music Vol. 2: The Age of Rock*, edited by Timothy E. Scheurer. Bowling Green, OH: Bowling Green State University Press, 1989, p. 129.
24. Robert Krout. "The Music Therapist as Singer-Songwriter: Applications with Bereaved Teenagers." In *Songwriting: Methods, Techniques, and Clinical Applications for Music Therapy*, edited by Felicity Baker and Tony Wigram. London: Jessica Kingsley, 2005, p. 214.
25. Pamela Phillips Oland. *The Art of Writing Great Lyrics*. New York: Allworth, 2001, p. 4.
26. Jason Blume. *Six Steps to Songwriting Success: The Comprehensive Guide to Writing and Marketing Hit Songs*. New York: Random House, 2004, p. 39.
27. Oland. *The Art of Writing Great Lyrics*, p. 3.
28. Rikky Rooksby. *Lyrics: Writing Better Words for Your Songs*. San Francisco: Backbeat, 2006, p. 97.
29. Jason Blume. *Inside Songwriting: Getting to the Heart of Creativity*. New York: Random House Digital, 2011.
30. Casey Kelly and David Hodge. *The Complete Idiot's Guide to the Art of Songwriting*, New York: Alpha, 2011, p. 69.
31. Kelly and Hodge. *The Complete Idiot's Guide to the Art of Songwriting*, p. 69.
32. Molly-Ann Leikin. *How to Be a Hit Songwriter: Polishing and Marketing Your Lyrics and Music*. Milwaukee, WI: Hal Leonard, 2003, p. 35.
33. Pat Luboff and Pete Luboff. *101 Songwriting Wrongs and How to Right Them: How to Craft and Sell Your Songs*. Cincinnati, OH: Writer's Digest, 2007, p. 63.

34. Luboff and Luboff. *101 Songwriting Wrongs and How to Right Them: How to Craft and Sell Your Songs*, p. 63.

Chapter 4: Putting the Pieces of a Song Together

35. Luboff and Luboff. *101 Songwriting Wrongs and How to Right Them: How to Craft and Sell Your Songs*, p. 54.

36. Michael Miller. *The Complete Idiot's Guide to Music Theory*, second edition. New York: Alpha, 2005, p. 108.

37. Miller. *The Complete Idiot's Guide to Music Theory*, p. 108.

38. John Stevens. *The Songs of John Lennon: The Beatles Years*. Boston: Berklee, 2002, p. 3.

39. Ralph Murphy. *Murphy's Laws of Songwriting: The Book*. Nashville, TN: Murphy Music Consulting, 2011, p. 124.

40. Kelly and Hodge. *The Complete Idiot's Guide to the Art of Songwriting*, p. 28.

41. Kelly and Hodge. *The Complete Idiot's Guide to the Art of Songwriting*, p. 28.

42. Michael Lydon. *Songwriting Success: How to Write Songs for Fun and (Maybe) Profit*. New York: Routledge, 2004, p. 66.

43. Eric Beall. *The Billboard Guide to Writing and Producing Songs That Sell: How to Create Hits in Today's Music Industry*. New York: Crown, 2009, p. 232.

44. Oland. *The Art of Writing Great Lyrics*, p. 3.

45. Rick Dean. "Writing Great Song Hooks." *Music Biz Brief*, January 10, 2012. http://thedeanofmusicpub lishing.com/musicbizblog/?p=25.

46. Jim Peterik, Dave Austin, and Cathy Lynn. *Songwriting for Dummies*, second edition. Hoboken, NJ: Wiley, 2010, p. 79.

47. Peterik, Austin, and Lynn. *Songwriting for Dummies*, p. 79.

Chapter 5: The Business of Songwriting

48. Dick Weissman. *Songwriting: The Words, the Music, and the Money*. Milwaukee, WI: Hal Leonard, 2001, p. viii.

49. Kelly and Hodge. *The Complete Idiot's Guide to the Art of Songwriting*, p. 136.

50. Shelly Field. *Career Opportunities in the Music Industry*, fifth edition. New York: Ferguson, 2004, p. 200.

51. Beall. *The Billboard Guide to Writing and Producing Songs That Sell: How to Create Hits in Today's Music Industry*, p. 9.

52. William Brohaugh and Adria Haley, eds. *2011 Songwriter's Market*, thirty-fourth edition. Cincinnati, OH: Writer's Digest, 2010, p. 8.

53. Sherry Bond. *The Songwriter's and Musician's Guide to Nashville*, third edition. New York: Allworth, 2004, p. 12.

54. Blume. *Six Steps to Songwriting Success: The Comprehensive Guide*

to Writing and Marketing Hit Songs, p. 170.

55. Steve Knopper. "How 10 Major Songwriters Make Big Money." *Rolling Stone*, January 19, 2012. www.rollingstone.com/music/pictures/how-10-major-songwriters-make-big-money-20120119.

56. Kenneth L. Fisher. *The Ten Roads to Riches: The Ways the Wealthy Got There (And How You Can, Too!)*. Hoboken, NJ: John Wiley & Sons, 2009.

57. Dick Weissman. *The Music Business: Career Opportunities and Self-Defense*, third edition. New York: Three Rivers, 2003.

Adele

19, 2008

One of the bestselling performers of modern times, award-winning soul singer Adele writes her own songs about her life experiences. *19*, her debut album, is about her life when she was age nineteen.

21, 2011

Tori Amos

Little Earthquakes, 1992

Known for writing moving, poetic lyrics for her piano-based rock songs, Amos debuted with this album in 1992.

Mariah Carey

Mariah Carey—Greatest Hits, 2001

Best known for her vocal range, award-winning pop singer Carey co-wrote many of the hits on this twenty-eight-track album.

Eric Clapton

Complete Clapton, 2007

This album includes thirty-six popular tracks from rock music star Clapton, fa-

mous for his singing, songwriting, and guitar playing.

Bob Dylan

The Essential Bob Dylan, 2000

This thirty-song compilation reflects some of the most notable songs of Bob Dylan's folk rock singing/songwriting career, spanning nearly four decades from the 1960s to the 1990s.

Peter Gabriel

New Blood, 2011

Songs from this award-winning singer-songwriter are given new twists on this album, which features unique rhythms and symphonic sounds.

Al Green

Greatest Hits, 2009

This album contains ten of this award-winning singer-songwriter's most popular 1970s soul singles.

Alan Jackson

34 Number Ones, 2010

This collection of thirty-four number one hits, many self-written or co-written, are featured on this album by one of the most popular country artists of the late 1990s and 2000s.

Michael Jackson

The Essential Michael Jackson, 2005

Jackson was one of the bestselling and award-winning musical performers of all time; he also had many writing and co-writing credits for his trademark hits, thirty-eight of which are on this album.

Mick Jagger

The Very Best of Mick Jagger, 2007

Jagger, lead singer of the rock band the Rolling Stones, is the writer or co-writer of the seventeen songs in this collection.

Jewel

Pieces of You, 1995

This genre-crossing album by singer-songwriter Jewel Kilcher became one of the bestselling debut albums of all time.

Elton John

Rocket Man—Number Ones, 2007

Along with co-writer Bernie Taupin, Elton John created these seventeen chart-topping rock and pop hits that have helped him sell more than 250 million records since the 1970s.

Alicia Keys

Songs in A Minor, 2001

Girl on Fire, 2012

The Grammy-winning pop artist says the songwriting element was instrumental in the creation of this album.

Carole King

Legendary Demos, 2012

A member of the Songwriters Hall of Fame, King wrote chart-topping songs for many artists beginning in the 1960s. This is a collection of thirteen of her original demo recordings that became smash hits.

Lady Gaga

Born This Way, 2011

Known for her outlandish stage outfits and style, Lady Gaga became a famous singer-songwriter in the 2000s.

John Lennon

Lennon Legend: The Very Best of John Lennon, 1998

This album features twenty of the best-known hits of the famed singer-songwriter who was originally one of the Beatles and later became an independent artist.

Bob Marley and the Wailers

Legend: The Best of Bob Marley and the Wailers, 2002

A member of the Songwriters Hall of Fame, Jamaican singer-songwriter

Bob Marley set trends in reggae music during his career spanning the 1960s and 1970s. This album has sixteen of his hits.

Dave Matthews Band

Under the Table and Dreaming, 1994

This debut album features the unique songwriting style of lead singer and guitarist Dave Matthews, whose alternative rock songs are known for unexpected rhythms, use of saxophones and violins, and unusual chord progressions.

Ne-Yo

In My Own Words, 2006

One of the most successful R&B artists of the 2000s, Ne-Yo has also written hit songs for other performing artists. This debut album marks his career transition from songwriter to singer-songwriter.

Nirvana

Nevermind, 1991

Kurt Cobain, lead singer of the 1990s grunge rock band Nirvana, was the writer/co-writer for all of the songs on this iconic album.

Brad Paisley

Hits Alive, 2010

This compilation album by award-winning country singer-songwriter Paisley contains twenty-five of his original songs, including many number-one country hits.

Bruce Springsteen

Born in the U.S.A., 1984

This album features some of Springsteen's most popular rock hits. He is known for writing songs with themes of everyday, common working people of America, which are showcased on this popular album originally released in 1984.

Taylor Swift

Taylor Swift, 2006

This bestselling, award-winning debut album features fifteen songs Swift wrote and performed when she debuted as a teen star in 2006.

James Taylor

Sweet Baby James, 1970

Greatest Hits, 2004

Taylor was one of the first artists to be labeled a singer-songwriter. His work in various genres—that spans more than four decades—is reflected in these twelve hits.

U2

U218 Singles, 2006

Paul David Hewson, popularly known as U2's lead singer Bono, has written songs for the award-winning alternative rock band that formed in Ireland in the late 1970s and is still successful today.

This album has eighteen of the group's biggest hits.

Gillian Welch

The Harrow and the Harvest, 2011

The folk artist shows off her songwriting skills in this album that was nominated for two Grammys.

Amy Winehouse

Back to Black, 2006

The Grammy-winning soul, jazz, and R&B singer-songwriter wrote and sang her own songs, some about her battle with substance abuse in the 2000s before her death from alcohol poisoning in 2011.

Stevie Wonder

Songs in the Key of Life, 1976

The Definitive Collection, 2002

Some of the biggest hits from the award-winning pop/R&B singer-songwriter's career, which began with a number-one hit in 1963 when he was thirteen, appear on this twenty-one-song album.

Neil Young

Greatest Hits, 2004

This album has sixteen of the singer-songwriter's biggest hits from a rock and folk music career that started in the 1960s and continues today.

GLOSSARY

alliteration: the repetition of the same letter or sound in a series of words.

chord: a group of notes, typically three, played together to create harmony in a song.

crescendo: an increase in the loudness or intensity of a song.

demo: a sample recording used to sell a song to people who might be interested in producing or recording it professionally.

harmony: a combination of musical notes that have a pleasing sound when played together.

hook: a catchy, often recurring part of a song that serves as its major memorable or repeatable part.

melody: a sequence of single notes that sound good together and make up a tune.

music publisher: the company that buys a songwriter's rights to a song and in return sells the song and pays the songwriter a portion of the profits.

record label: a company that makes and markets professional recordings of songs.

rhythm: a strong, repeated pattern of sound.

royalty: payments for the use of one's creative work, usually a percentage of each sale.

syncopation: a temporary shift in emphasis of a song's rhythm.

tempo: the speed at which a song or a part of a song is played.

FOR MORE INFORMATION

Books

Dave Austin, Jim Peterik, and Cathy Lynn. *Songwriting for Dummies*, second edition. Hoboken, NJ: Wiley, 2010. With chapters on lyrics, melody, song genres, and publishing, this book provides tips on all the major aspects of songwriting with easy explanations for novices.

Robin Frederick. *Shortcuts to Hit Songwriting: 126 Proven Techniques for Writing Songs That Sell*. Calabasas, CA: TAXI Music, 2008. This book, well suited for people just starting out in songwriting, discusses how to learn from hit songs, choose genres, find good ideas, and understand song structures that work.

Pat Pattinson. *Writing Better Lyrics: The Essential Guide to Powerful Songwriting*, second edition. Cincinnati, OH: Writers Digest, 2010. This book explores many aspects of lyric writing, from rhyming and rhythm to point of view. The author teaches college lyric-writing courses, and his students have included Grammy winners John Mayer and Gillian Welch.

J. Douglas Waterman, ed. *Song: The World's Best Songwriters on Creating the Music That Moves Us*. Cincinnati, OH: Writers Digest, 2007. This compilation includes interviews from one hundred songwriters in varying genres, including Kenny Chesney, Rob Thomas, and Sheryl Crow. In their own words, they discuss the art and business of songwriting.

Articles

Cliff Goldmacher. "Five Myths About Achieving Success as a Songwriter." Broadcast Music, March 27, 2012. www.bmi.com/news/entry/five _myths_about_achieving_success_ as_a_songwriter. A songwriter and producer explores five common misconceptions songwriters often have about the industry and making a career out of their craft.

John Jurgensen. "The Secrets of Songwriters." *Wall Street Journal*, August 13, 2010. http://online.wsj.com /article/SB1000142405274870416490 4575421813516451790.html. This article discusses how modern songwriters create relevant songs in a rapidly changing world.

Jonathan Widran. "Hitmaker Ryan Tedder Leads His Band OneRepublic, Writes Hits for Leona Lewis,

Beyoncé, Kelly Clarkson." Songwriter Universe, 2010. www.songwriteruniverse.com/ryantedder123.htm. The article explains how the lead singer of OneRepublic, who is also an award-winning songwriter for some of pop music's biggest stars, balances the two aspects of his career.

Websites

American Songwriter (www.americansongwriter.com). This site provides links to recent issues of *American Songwriter* magazine as well as information about the craft of songwriting, new technology songwriters use, important developments in music, and more.

Songwriters Resource Network (www.songwritersresourcenetwork.com). This news and education-centered site for songwriters and composers has articles, networking opportunities, and information about events for songwriters to learn more about the craft, hone their skills, and network with others.

The Songwriting School of Los Angeles (http://thesongwritingschool.com). This site provides links and information about the school's many online classes for learning songwriting, as well as links to blogs, networking opportunities, and other free information.

TAXI (www.taxi.com). This site contains information about all aspects of music writing and publishing as well as networking opportunities and links to helpful books and resources.

INDEX

A

AABA song form, 67
Adele, 51, 90, *94*
African Americans, 15, 24, 25–26, 28
African American music, 24–25
Alliteration, 60
American Idol (TV show), 81
Amplifiers, 22, *86*
Award-winning songs, 91–93, *94*

B

Backbeat, 41, 43
Bass guitars, 22, 24, 44, 45
Beatboxers/beatboxing, *44,* 44–45
The Beatles, 12, *13*, 24, 67, 68
Beauchamp, G.D., 22
"Big Yellow Taxi" (song), 51
Billboard (magazine), 25, *25*, 66
Blues music, 19, 23, 25–26, 30
   See also Rhythm and blues (R&B)
Bridges (song element), 68
Brown, James, 28, *29*

C

Carson, Johnny, *29*
Chords (music), 32, 35–39, *38*, *46*
Choruses (song element), 53–54, 68
Civil War (U.S.), 20, 24
Clarkson, Kelly, 81
Classical music, 7, 15, 31–32, 41, 46
Compact discs (CDs), 7, 84
Composers, 6, 9, 31–32

Composition

Composition, 6, *46*
Computers, 84, 85, *86*
Country music
   geographical differences, 14, 22–23
   modern, 20–21, *21*
   overview, 19
   roots, 19–20
Crosby, Bing, 12

D

Dance/dancing
   community and, 19
   in disco era, 12, 28
   funk and, *29*
   songs for, 26, 40, 41, 43, 48, 65
Dance music (genre), 7, 25
Daughtry, Chris, 81
Demos, 84–85
Digital music files, 78, 79, 84–85
Disco music, 12, 28, 40
The-Dream (songwriter), *50*
Drum sets, 22, 43–44
Drums, 24, 42–45

E

Edison, Thomas, 16, *16*
Electric guitars, 22–24, *23*, 31
Eminem, *58*

F

Film scores, 47

First-person narration, 50–51, 52–93
Flat notes, 33
Folk tales, 49
Foster, Mark, 78
Foster, Stephen, 18
Foster the People, 66, 78, *78*
Four-beat rhythm, 41
Fresh, Doug E., *44*
Funk music, 28–29, *29*, 40
Furtado, Nelly, 56, *57*

G

Grammy Awards, 93, *94*
Great Depression, 18
Greek muses, 6
Guitars, 20, 22, 37, *38*, 86

H

Haley, Bill, 41
Hand-beaten drums, 43–44
Harmonies, 6, 35–36, 42, 45, 46, 72–73
Hip-hop, 25, 44, *58*
    See also Rap
Home note, 36
Hooks (song element), 55, 74–77

I

Ideas in songwriting, 63–66
Instrumental music, 22, 48
iTunes, 25, *88*

J

James, Rick, 28
Jazz, 12, 22, 26, 30, 48
Jepsen, Carley Rae, 60, *61*
Jingles, 55
Jobs, Steve, *88*
John, Elton, *64*

L

Legend, John, *92*
Lennon, John, 64, 67, 68
    See also Beatles, The
Levine, Adam, *43*
Lincoln, Abraham, 20
Lyrics
    overview, 47, 48
    pitfalls in, 59–61
    pronounceable words, 58–59
    structure, 52–54
    telling stories through, 48–52, 67
    well-polished words, 62
    word rhythms, 56–58

M

Major key, 32
Manson, Marilyn, 24
Maroon 5, 42, *43*
McCartney, Paul, 64, 67
    See also Beatles, The
McGraw, Tim, 52
Measures (music), 41, 45–46
Melodic phrase, 54, 67
Melodies, 6, 9, 33–35, 46, 73
Metaphors, in songwriting, 56, 57
Microphones, 85–86, *86*
Minor key, 32
Mitchell, Joni, 51, *51*
Motown music, 26–28, *27*
"Moves Like Jagger" (song), 42
Music
    elements, 6, 31–32, 40, 45, 64
    history of American music, 15–19
    notes, 9, 22, 32, 33, 42, 34
    recording industry, 16
    as storytelling device, 9–11
    *See also specific musical terms and song
        elements*
Music publishers, 83, 87

N

Nasal tones, 61
National Academy of Recording Arts and
  Sciences, 93
Newman, Randy, *47*
Nichols, Tim, 52

O

One-hit wonders, 90–91
Open vowel sounds, 61

P

Pearl Jam, 78
Perry, Katy, 77
Phonograph, *16*, 18–19
Piano notes, 33–34
Piano tunes, 17, 22
Poetry and songwriting, 54–56, 82
Pop music
  changing phenomenon of, 14–15
  history, 12–13
  musical elements in, 32
  song forms, 67
  Tin Pan Alley and, 14
Presley, Elvis, 60
Professional recording studios, 86

Q

Queen (musical group), 76, 78

R

Ragtime music, 17, 22
Rap music, 12, 28–30, 45, 58–59, 73
  See also Hip-hop
Rascal Flatts, 20, *56*
Recording equipment, 85–86, *86*
Recording industry, 16, 18
Religious music, 15, 28
Rihanna, 50, *50*, 90

R

Rhyming, 54–56
Rhythm
  in musical compositions, *46*
  good beats, 41–42
  making of, 42–45
  overview, 6, 9
  predictability in, 73
  as song's heartbeat, 39–40
Rhythm and blues (R&B), 15, 19, 28–30,
  29, 59
Rickenbacker, Adolph, 22
Rock music
  development, 19, 22–23, *23*
  geographical differences, 22
  Motown and soul music and, 26–28, *27*
  popularity, 23–24
  rhythm and blues (R&B) and, 15, 19,
    28–30, *29*
Rogers, Kenny, 52
Royalties, 88–90

S

Schlitz, Don, 52
Second-person narration, 51
Sharp notes, 33
Sheet music, 7, 14, 16, *17*, 45–47, *46*
Similes in songwriting, 56
Slavery, 18, 20
Smith, Will, *44*
Song credit, 90
Songs
  attention-grabbing, 74–77
  character growth and change in, 69–70
  choruses, 53–54, 68
  climaxes, 68
  expectations in, 70–72
  ideas, 63–66
  initial beats, 42
  moods, 32
  names of, 77–79
  pop song forms, 67
  shapes, 66–69

standouts, 72–74
verses, 53–54, 58
See also Lyrics; *specific musical terms*
and song elements
Songwriters
claiming status as, 71
collaborations, 64
in pop music, 13
as students of musical history, 19
See also specific people and musical
genres
Songwriters Hall of Fame (SHoF), 92
Songwriting
careers in, 11
culture of writing in song, 8–11
ideas, 63–66
learning the craft, 80–82
overview, 63
poetry and, 54–56, 82
sheet music and, 45–47, *46*
skills, 84–86
See also Lyrics; Songs
Songwriting business
award-winning songs, 91–93, *94*
copyrights, 83
economic reality of, 89–90
digital advancements and, 85
future of, 94–95
overview, 80
royalties and ownership, 88–90
selling songs, 87–88
sharing songs, 82–84
success in, 15
Soul music, 26–28
Spalding, Esperanza, *37*

Stressed syllables, 58
Sugarhill Gang, 29
The Supremes (musical group), *27*, 28
Swift, Taylor, 20, *21,* 51, 60
Syncopation, 41–42, 45, 73–75

T

Taupin, Bernie, *64*
Tempo, 68, 73
The Temptations (musical group), *27*, 28
Third-person narration, 52
Tin Pan Alley, 14
Tongue-twisting lyrics, 29, 60

U

U.S. Copyright Office, 83

V

Vega, Suzanne, 52
Verses (song element), 53–54, 58
The Voice (TV show), 81

W

Waltzes, 41
"We Will Rock You" (song), 76
West, Kanye, *92*
Wiseman, Craig, 52

X

The X Factor (TV show), 81

PICTURE CREDITS

Jenny MacKay has written more than twenty nonfiction books for kids and teens on topics like crime scene investigation, sports science, and technology. She lives with her husband, son, and daughter in Sparks, Nevada, where she listens to all kinds of music, from country to rap and rock.